A GUIDE TO
JEWISH PRACTICE

ORGANIZATIONAL
ETHICS
AND ECONOMIC
JUSTICE

A GUIDE
to JEWISH
PRACTICE

Center for Jewish Ethics
Reconstructionist Rabbinical College
in cooperation with the
Reconstructionist Rabbinical Association

Reconstructionist Rabbinical College Press

1299 Church Road, Wyncote, PA 19095-1898
www.rrc.edu

ORGANIZATIONAL ETHICS
AND ECONOMIC
JUSTICE

DAVID A. TEUTSCH

Reconstructionist Rabbinical College Press
Wyncote, Pennsylvania

Composition by G&H Soho, Inc.

ISBN 978-0-938945-12-3

                                                              2005935343

Printed in the U.S.A.

Contents

In honor of Adam Schesch
and his Tree of Life project,
which helped to launch the RRC Ethics Center,
its courses and early publication.

Commentators

Adina Abramowitz (A.A.)
Joseph N. Cohen (J.N.C.)
Fred Scherlinder Dobb (F.S.D.)
Dan Ehrenkrantz (D.E.)
Richard Hirsh (R.H.)
Leah Kamionkowski (L.K.)
Tamar Kamionkowski (T.K.)
Myriam Klotz (M.K.)
Nina H. Mandel (N.H.M.)

Deborah Dash Moore (D.D.M.)
Mark Nussbaum (M.N.)
Nancy Post (N.P.)
Yael Ridberg (Y.R.)
Luis Schuchinski (L.S.)
Jacob J. Staub (J.J.S.)
David A. Teutsch (D.A.T.)
Sheila Peltz Weinberg (S.P.W.)
Edward D. Zinbarg (E.Z.)

Advisory Committee

Rabbis Richard Hirsh and David Teutsch, *Co-chairs*
Rabbi Lester Bronstein
Deborah Dash Moore, Ph.D.
Chayim Herzig-Marx
Leah Kamionkowski
Rabbi Nina Mandel
Rabbi Yael Ridberg
Rabbi Jacob Staub

Preface

Our lives are profoundly affected by organizations and their conduct. Following the guidance this volume provides in economic, business and organizational matters can have a major impact on people's lives.

This sixth section of *A Guide to Jewish Practice* represents another step in completing this Guide to practice for contemporary Jews. Other books will follow soon.

The diligent and thoughtful work of the *Guide*'s Advisory Committee and commentators are essential to the success of this project. Their advice has substantially improved the text, and all remaining faults are mine. Cheryl Plumly has again taken responsibility for the manuscript. Marilyn Silverstein handled proofreading. Jennifer Abraham provided technical support. Jim Harris and his team at G & H Soho did the typesetting and production.

This book is dedicated to Adam Schesch, one of the first supporters of the Ethics Center, who showed faith in its possibilities when it had not yet started to bear fruit. The funding for this volume comes from the Levin-Lieber program in Jewish ethics of the Reconstructionist Rabbinical College. I am grateful to Dan Levin for his ongoing support and friendship.

David A. Teutsch

ORGANIZATIONAL ETHICS
AND ECONOMIC
JUSTICE

Many of our encounters with other people are commercial in nature. People buy and sell things, work together on business projects, negotiate contracts, supervise employees and receive supervision, enforce agreements that have financial implications, hire plumbers and pay doctor bills. People often pay fees to use gyms, attend programs and park cars. Every time that people travel, work, shop or see an advertisement, they are caught up in some form of commerce. The ethics of commerce, business and organizations are tightly intertwined with each other and with the concerns of economic justice. Whether we work in a business, volunteer for a not-for-profit organization, or simply go to the store, there are ethical components to the way we make decisions and undertake our tasks.

Martin Buber's classical presentation of human relationships as "I-It" or "I-Thou" reminds us that notwithstanding the commercial or economic nature of a transaction, we always have a choice as to the attitude we bring toward the person with whom we are interacting.   —R.H.

Framing the Issues

In modern society, the individual is seen as the fundamental social unit, and the assumption of capitalism has been that the way to maximize economic production and distribution is through "the invisible hand" of unfettered markets. That assumption rests on the belief that the primary motive of individuals is to seek the greatest economic benefit. Many of the dilemmas and problems that grow out of unrestrained capitalism have been tempered by government regulations such as the ones that regulate the purity of food and drugs, place limits on the conduct of financial markets, establish safety standards for the workplace, limit pollution, ensure fair competition and prevent excessive profits by legitimate monopolies (such as water, electric and natural gas companies). These regulations are critically important in improving the economic life in Western

It is not only capitalism that raises moral dilemmas. All economic systems, however laudatory their principles may be, are administered and applied by fallible human beings. Humanity has yet to devise an economic system capable of producing equality of opportunity and achievement. The Torah aptly captures this gap between "ought" and "is" in these contrasting verses: "There shall be no needy among you . . . if only you heed God . . ." (Deuteronomy. 15:4), and "There will never cease to be needy ones in your land" (Deuteronomy 15:11).   —R.H.

Unfettered capitalism was never categorically supported by Adam Smith, the pre-eminent philosophical defender of market forces. Smith clearly recognized the need for state intervention when the market did not operate properly—in cases, for example, where businessmen were out-and-out crooks. The "neo-Darwinist" strain in Smith's thought is softened by his parallel emphasis on the empathic behavior that underlies social intercourse.   —J.N.C.

This emphasis on the primacy of the individual as a social unit is in sharp contrast to the concept of Jewish peoplehood, in which the interests of the individual—economic as well as social—are closely linked to the maintenance and survival of the local and the global Jewish community.   —N.H.M.

democracies, but they do not shift the stress that is placed on the individual as worker and consumer. Thus the individual remains the primary economic engine and unit of distribution. The common way of summarizing this approach to business is that "it's a dog-eat-dog world" where it is the responsibility of the buyer to beware, or, as the Latin catch phrase has it, *caveat emptor.*

Because capitalism raises so many moral dilemmas, Jews have been leaders in considering both communism and socialism. Both of these approaches have demonstrated their own flaws, particularly around issues of fair decision making and the efficient production and distribution of goods. Most of the energy within Jewish tradition around questions of the production and distribution of goods has been focused on resolving the moral challenges of market economies. This reflects the predominance of

Another control on the individualism of the capitalist system is the concept of "public goods" put forward by Mancur Olson (in *The Logic of Collective Action: Public Goods and the Theory of Groups*). Public goods are goods that society benefits from or agrees that we need, but no one person can afford to pay for them, so we agree to pay for them collectively through taxes. Common public goods include roads, schools and the army. As our society has changed, the political and social agreements about what constitutes a public good have also changed. Recently we have seen that political willingness to fund the military is considerably greater than the willingness to upgrade the levees in New Orleans, for example. In Jewish life we pay for public goods through dues to support our congregations, communal donations and fees.   —A.A.

European socialist norms place a higher burden of responsibility on society for the welfare of groups—the elderly, children, the infirm and so on. Public policy in the U.S. is often less socially responsive than other Western democracies.   —N.P.

Jews have done more than "consider" communism and socialism. They have supported both movements, they have articulated ways to blend socialism with democracy and with Zionism, and they have implemented both small-scale and large-scale efforts to create a classless and just society in Europe, North and South America, and especially in Israel.   —D.D.M.

market economies, the inability of Jews to create entirely different alternatives in the real world and, perhaps most important, the ongoing Jewish expectation that the moral difficulties produced by unregulated market economies can be effectively dealt with by a combination of legal and moral regulation.

Three root attitudes of Judaism suggest a direction far different from unconstrained capitalism. The first is *"avadim hayinu lefaro bemitzrayim,* we were slaves to Pharaoh in Egypt" (Deuteronomy 6:21). Since we know what it is like to be treated unfairly, we should act with empathy and a sense for justice. While many people who have been treated badly see that as a justification for treating others badly, that approach has never been acceptable within Judaism. All forms of *ona'a* (oppression) are uneth-

---

The historical circumstances of marginal living, enforced second-class status and prohibitions against Jewish business and land ownership most likely inclined Jews in Eastern Europe to gravitate toward more egalitarian and idealistic economic models.

—N.H.M.

The purpose of most economic and financial market regulation is to legislate fairness—to level the playing field so that no party to a transaction has an unfair economic advantage over another party. But what is fair? In most cases, it means requiring full disclosure of all pertinent information, not permitting one party to use an informational advantage to gain an improper advantage over the other party. We call this "transparency"—and many rules and regulations are in place to ensure that both the buyer and the seller engage in transparent behavior. If you desire to behave ethically, the simple principle of treating others as you yourself would like to be treated is the ultimate benchmark.   —M.N.

Remembering that we were slaves shifts our understanding of what it means to be free. When the Israelites were liberated from Egypt, they were "freed" from oppression, but it took wandering through the wilderness and building a just society to understand what it truly meant to be a "free people." Even then, it took much trial, rebellion and tribulation. Freedom from oppression must translate into the responsibility and obligation to treat others with the same openness and commitment to their freedom.   —Y.R.

ical (see Exodus 22:20–26). This moral principle is binding even if a particular act of oppression is not illegal. The early rabbis who shaped rabbinic tradition (hereafter, "the rabbis") also taught that remembering we were slaves should remind us that we could become slaves again. No matter how secure a person may be, anyone can lose everything and survive only through the mercy of others. This realization should motivate people to treat others with fairness and empathy and to act to ensure their welfare. When we act based on empathy and a sense of fairness, we are not only ensuring the welfare of the person before us, we are also doing what we can to ensure our own future welfare, and if not our own, then perhaps that of some of our loved ones.

The second fundamental Jewish attitude that shapes economic life is that we are tenants in the world, not owners. "*Ladonay ha'aretz umelo'o,* the earth and all that is in it belong to God," proclaims the psalmist (Psalms 24:1).

Many professional associations establish codes of conduct—standards of behavior—for interactions with clients, so that clients can expect that individuals who identify themselves as professionals will conduct themselves in a certain manner. These associations are self-regulated, with censorship and loss of certification the ultimate punishments for failure to adhere to those standards.   —M.N.

"No matter how secure a person may be, anyone can lose everything . . ." While this is true in a narrow sense as a hypothetical, in a wider perspective the universality of mortality ought to influence our desire to accumulate beyond what we need because one day, each of us will inevitably leave behind all that we have acquired.   —R.H.

Empathy is a universal human need with the power to connect the infinitely diverse human race.   —S.P.W.

Psalms 24:1 figures prominently in liberation theology. For this progressive religious movement of the past four decades or so, initially from Catholic Latin America, the rallying cry is "*De Jehova es la tierra, y su plenitude* (Psalms 24:1)": nature's wealth belongs not to multinational corporations or ruling elites, but to God, who loves the *campesino* and the *Presidente* equally.   —F.S.D.

We have an obligation to respect the wishes of the Owner, so we cannot do whatever we like with the property. The implications of this idea are broad. Perhaps the most obvious is that just as a tenant is not allowed to deface the apartment or office she rents, so we are not allowed to damage the environment intentionally and irreparably. Our tradition extends this notion much further, however. It suggests that the wealth of the world should be used on behalf of all its inhabitants. While Genesis describes humanity as having dominion over other creatures, Jewish ethics has never seen that dominion as having no limits; we are also stewards of the world with responsibility for it. In a world where there is enough for everyone to eat, allowing anyone to go hungry is a violation of our stew-

Countless "native" traditions hold that we are stewards of the earth rather than its owners.
—N.P.

"We have an obligation to respect the wishes of the Owner . . ." This would be considerably easier if we believed that scripture accurately records the Owner's intent! Insofar as Reconstructionist Judaism understands the words of scripture to be human words reaching out for the divine in life, we ought to be cautious about asserting certitude about what the "Owner" would have us do.   —R.H.

In Hebrew there is no word that can be directly translated into "owner" or "ownership." Things can "belong" (*shayakhut*) to someone. One can be a "master" (*ba'al*) over something. But ownership as we understand it in English can refer only to the One owner— God—and we are merely stewards.   —Y.R.

Genesis describes humanity as having both dominion and the responsibilities of stewardship. These two attitudes are brought into relationship with each other in the very first biblical book.   —D.E.

Rashi, the 11th century scholar, comments on Genesis 1:26 that whatever dominion we have is conditional. Where Genesis says that God planned to create humans "in our image" and to "let them rule over (*yir'du*)" the rest of Creation, Rashi interprets, "If they merit, let them rule (*rodeh*); if not, let them fall (*yarud*)." A century later, Maimonides (*Moreh Nevukhim* 3.13) would say of Genesis that "dominion" is descriptive of a capacity in human nature, rather than prescriptive of the human role in the universe. We do not have an unconditional mandate to dominate.   —F.S.D.

ardship as the rabbis understand it. From a Jewish perspective, commitment to the just distribution of resources is the result of understanding the rights and obligations inherent in being human.

The third framing Jewish attitude is that human beings are created *b'tzelem Elohim,* in the image of God (Genesis 1:26). The infinite worth of human beings means that they should not be reduced to being means to an end, like rowers in a slave galley. Each of us reflects the divine presence in the world, so we must see each person we encounter— bus driver or salesperson, student or teacher, executive or janitor—as a person worthy of our recognition, attention, caring and commitment. This should shape every one of our encounters with others, as it should shape the rules and procedures that we use in our economic lives.

Martin Buber suggests that we encounter other individuals as created *b'tzelem Elohim,* that we establish "I-Thou" relationships with them. In doing so, we see beyond the extraneous and utilitarian aspects of the other person and connect deeply. By contrast, when we engage others for what we can get from them, they become objects in our eyes. This defines an I-It relationship. Buber asserts that most people cannot constantly sustain I-Thou attention. We move between I-Thou moments and I-It ways in which we engage the world. Jewish wisdom encourages us to stretch beyond the illusion of separation between self and others, and to safeguard the dignity and well-being of each person even when we are not able to sustain deep attention to their fundamental essence.
—M.K.

Identifying *tzelem Elohim* as the core Jewish value that it is may seem radical and utopian. However, it gives direction and depth to our efforts in many domains—spiritual as well as political and economic.   —S.P.W.

Some "native" traditions value *all* life (animal, plant and human) as an aspect of a divine intent. Consequently, humans are considered different from other elements in the natural world.   —N.P.

Three values central to economic ethics grow out of these attitudes. The first is the emphasis placed on *kehila,* community. It suggests that the welfare of a community as a whole is of primary importance. Economic transactions should be done in ways that strengthen the interpersonal ties on which community is based and that serve the needs of the community as a whole.

The second value is *emet* (truth). Truth is central to how people relate to each other. This concept is explored fully in the *Ethics of Speech* section of *A Guide to Jewish Practice.* Since trust is critical to community and trust rests in part on

---

These three Jewish attitudes are comprehensive. If I had to add one more, it would be *V'ahavta l'reyakha kamokha,* "You shall love your neighbor as yourself" (Leviticus 19:18). Maybe that is the essence of empathy.   —S.P.W.

As *parashat Nitzavim* in Deuteronomy reminds us, "You stand this day, all of you . . . from woodchopper to water drawer, to enter into the covenant of your God" (Deuteronomy 29:9–11). Hierarchies shaped by profession, class and caste have nothing to do with our spiritual standing, our essential worth, or our God-given inalienable rights.   —F.S.D.

These values embody not only a communitarian perspective. They clearly reflect the Jewish emphasis on an ethics that sees what is good as stemming not just from the maximization of non-moral value but from what is just or what God demands in combination with a pragmatic appreciation of the importance of consequences in determining right actions. As the philosopher Immanuel Kant put it, the moral worth of an action does not reside "in the purpose to be attained by it, but in the maxim in accordance with which it is decided upon."   —J.N.C.

How does conspicuous consumption fit with our sense of Jewish values? The individual is required to make ethical choices about both how to accumulate wealth and what to do with it. Regardless of how the wealth was generated, is the community better served by your purchase of a new, expensive, imported automobile, or by your gift to the education fund? Achieving balance is the constant life struggle for each individual desiring to live ethically. Learning to draw the line between living well and living excessively is an individual challenge that we each must face.   —M.N.

The biblical prophets knew that a healthy economy is a necessary part of a healthy society as a whole. Zechariah 8:12–13 expresses this eloquently: "What the people sows shall prosper. The vine shall produce its fruit, the ground shall produce its yield, and . . . you shall become a blessing."   —T.K.

truth and integrity, a commitment to *emet* plays a major role in ethical business practice, as it does in ethics more broadly.

The third value, *kavod* (honor), involves the recognition and preservation of human dignity. Preserving the *kavod* of workers, consumers and business partners is a powerful guiding value of Jewish ethics. An economic system that undermines human dignity is immoral.

These attitudes and values together are excellent predictors of the positions that Jewish commercial ethics takes on the many issues to which we must respond. However, the development of Jewish ethics is also pragmatic. People need to be able to earn a living, to exist in the world economy, and to respond to changing external conditions. This has led some people to confuse business ethics with legal compli-

---

I heard Rabbi Michael Strassfeld teach that the word *emet* is composed of the first and last letters of the Hebrew alphabet and one very close to the middle. There is no single middle letter, though, teaching us that the heart of the truth that humans can grasp is still only an approximation. We need to struggle to bring forth the closest thing to truth of which we are capable.   —M.K.

Human dignity is of such importance that it overrides a negative commandment found in the Torah (B. Talmud *Berakhot* 19b).   —L.K.

Preserving the *kavod* of workers is paramount. Many organizations are forced to "right size" as a result of changing economic conditions. *Kavod* means exercising care and respect in letting people go. Involuntarily losing one's job is a traumatic experience, and the employer has an ethical obligation to do it as caringly as possible. This includes *what* is said and *how* it is said to both the individual and the general public. Rather than saying publicly, "We are pruning our organization to get rid of our dead wood," the employer should say, "We are refocusing our business, and unfortunately had to let a lot of very good and valuable people go." Providing outplacement assistance is the sign of an enlightened employer and a way to provide both workers and the community with the proper *kavod*.   —M.N.

Rabbi Yohanan said, "Jerusalem was destroyed because its inhabitants based their judgments on the law of the Torah." That is, they based their judgments strictly on the laws of the Torah and did not go *lifnim meshurat hadin* (beyond the narrow requirements of the law) (B. Talmud *Bava Metzia* 30b).   —L.K./F.S.D.

ance. Ethical conduct often has requirements that go beyond the law, which Jewish tradition describes as *lifnim meshurat hadin* (beyond the strict requirement of law). Rabbinic decisions about business practices were tempered by an awareness of what is possible in the marketplace, but the rabbis differentiated between *halakha* (Jewish law) on the one hand and ethical standards on the other. In arriving at their ethical perspective, they balanced their ideals with their sense of what was reasonable given the world within which they were living. That balancing act continues in our time. People who are more secure financially often have a greater capacity to withstand any negative economic consequences that result from adhering to high ethical standards. Given that most Jews are economically far better off than our ancestors, it should be easier than it used to be to ensure that ethical considerations receive their full weight in our judgments.

This is the difference between "what can I get away with" and "what ought I to do."
—R.H.

Ethical living requires balancing in a way that is both practical and fair to oneself. We all make our own decisions, and one purpose of education should be to provide healthy grounding in good decision making. The balancing act is highly tested when one is under severe pressure or multiple constraints. In recent years many prominent business executives have engaged in unethical, illegal and often criminal conduct. Some of them say that they did not realize how wrong their conduct was at the time they were doing it and that they were influenced by the demands of the moment. In some cases they were not acting for obvious personal gain. Their balancing act or moral compass failed them.   —L.S.

Most respected organizations recognize the value of ethical behavior toward their employees and provide incentive plans to share the economic rewards more broadly. However, one should ensure that the distribution is fair and not forget the risks of unequal distribution. Excesses in the arena of executive compensation and "perks" to the detriment of all stakeholders have been widely publicized. If the distribution is perceived to be unfair, the decision can be harmful to others in addition to being unethical. Ensuring fairness and more equal distribution should be primary motivations.   —M.N.

Sh'mita *and Jubilee*

The Torah describes two methods of redistribution. Every seventh year (*sh'mita*), Jewish slaves were set free and debts forgiven (Deuteronomy 15:12–15). These Jewish slaves were people who had sold themselves or were sold as children because of economic necessity. In the 50ᵗʰ (*yovel* /Jubilee) year, property that had been sold was supposed to revert to its original owner according to the tribal allocations established when the Israelites first entered their land (Leviticus 25:15–16).

However wealthy we may be, complacency should not blind us to the matrix of forces beyond us—luck, God, nature, other people—upon which our successes are utterly dependent. A bloated sense of entitlement distorts our self-understanding and obscures our obligations to others. We should consciously minimize what privilege we enjoy today and seek to extend it to others.   —F.S.D.

While the relative wealth of Jewish individuals is certainly evidenced by statistical and anecdotal evidence, poverty can—and does—exist in Jewish communities. Despite the ideals of our tradition, there are Jews oppressed by poverty in the most prevalent categories: the elderly, unskilled laborers, immigrants and single-parent families.   —N.H.M.

The Torah's two methods of redistribution have always impressed me as a remarkable prefiguring of modern progressive thought. While there are concerns about the practicality of these measures, and thus questions as to how widely they were implemented, the moral principles they embody reinforce an overall commitment to economic redistribution as a necessary component in the creation of a just society.   —J.N.C.

When a new king was crowned in Mesopotamia, he would declare a general forgiveness of all debts and the release of slaves. Our ancestors adopted this practice, but separated it from a king's declaration. Instead, the law was understood as coming from God and was set every 50 years regardless of the ruler in place.   —T.K.

While *yovel* imagines a genuine redistribution of property, the seventh-year elimination of debt and freeing of slaves seems to me to be more of a restoration than a redistribution.   —R.H.

Of course, the *yovel* did not mean that everyone would have ended up with the same amount of land, since some families grew and others shrank and the tribes changed size overall, as well. While it is unclear whether these methods of redistribution were ever actually employed,

While we will never know whether the regulations of *sh'mita* and *yovel* were ever implemented, their survival in the Torah has profound implications. The principle that underlies them is that all inequities of economic class are deviations from the ideal. The divine intent, according to the Torah, is that all such inequities must be rectified regularly. While historical evidence shows clearly that Jewish communities through the generations have accepted and reinforced class differences, such precedents have no authoritative power—not if the Torah states explicitly that we are periodically commanded to see through economic inequity to the will of God that we all be equal.   —J.J.S.

It is instructive to distinguish between principles like *sh'mita* and Jubilee that originally applied only to the Jewish community and the principles that have always been more universal in scope, like *kavod*. The ethical principles enunciated in the Torah contain some of both. As a child, I was impressed by the moral imperative for Jews to welcome strangers and the needy into their homes for the Passover seder, an imperative that I always assumed applied to both Jews and non-Jews alike. While the original rabbinic understanding was that the seder invitation applied only to Jews, many have expanded it to include non-Jews, illustrating a process of a broadened application of our values and principles that has paralleled our economic and social integration.   —J.N.C.

Even assuming a relatively long life, the Jubilee's 50-year interval means that redistribution would take place at most once during a person's lifetime.   —D.D.M.

Practicality aside, the *yovel*/Jubilee model is a brilliant synthesis of capitalism and socialism, retaining the best of both worlds. The theory of the Jubilee was that people would have an incentive to build up society and the economy by pursuing their own profits, knowing that they could keep a good percentage—for a while. But to the extent that the "original" distribution of land was just and would not subsequently have been made unjust by differential birthrates, every 50 years the playing field would be leveled, returning the means of production to the broadest number of people. Intergenerational inequities would not fester and deepen; equality of opportunity would be guaranteed; and all the while the land and the rest of Creation would enjoy a sustainable break, as well. We would do well to reintroduce some version of Jubilee today.   —F.S.D.

We know ourselves. We know moments of invisibility, of being spurned, judged, cast to the side or the rear. We know how deep a wound can be. Our willingness not to do to the other what is hateful to ourselves can ignite the willingness to redistribute power and ownership.   —S.P.W.

even with their flaws and potential inequities they represent a profound commitment to justice (see Deuteronomy 15:7–11). Extremely unequal distribution of resources prevents people from maintaining a dignified place in society. The guarantee of redistribution would mean that people could look forward to a time when they could begin again. The opportunity to live in dignity and pursue one's self-interest is essential to Jewish notions of justice.

The Dignity of Work

Jewish tradition teaches that work is a source of *kavod*. When we have done our economic share, we have a different relationship to what we consume. The idea that labor is a critical source of human dignity has powerful biblical and rabbinic support. The rabbis required fathers

While the promise of property redistribution may have been encouraging in principle, I wonder how encouraging it might have been to wait 50 years for property redistribution in a time when the average life span was probably less than that. Biblical promises have a way of sounding reassuring with the luxury of hindsight, but in the case of those who died before their fulfillment, such promises were hollow. It may be reassuring to hear that "your descendents will be slaves in Egypt for 400 years, but then I will come and free them," but in the meantime a lot of people lived and died as slaves. I am more inclined to think that such promises are criteria against which to measure our discontent with what is—and therefore motivate us to improve things—rather than assurances of what will be.   —R.H.

The God in whose image we are created is pictured, from the very first chapter of Genesis, as a working God, one who creates on every one of the first six days—and then creates daily, as is stated in the first blessing of the morning service—*hameḥadesh betuvo bekhol yom tamid ma'asey v'reyshit*, "who in goodness renews the work of creation every day." Some people picture perfection as immutable. Not the Jews. Thank God that God does finally rest on the seventh day, reminding us that rest, as well as work, is godly.   —J.J.S.

From *Pirkey Avot* 3:17 we learn that "where there is no flour, there is no Torah; where there is no Torah, there is no flour." This reminds us that worldly needs (flour) and spiritual needs (Torah) must be met in balance with each other.   —N.H.M.

to teach their sons a trade; we would broaden this to include all parents and all children. "You will eat the fruit of your labor and be happy, and it will be well with you" says the psalmist (Psalms 128:2). The Talmud (*Berakhot* 8A) interprets this verse to mean "happy" in this world and "well with you" in the world to come, and goes on to point out that reverence for God (*yirat Shamayim*) does not by itself guarantee that things will go well in the next world. Work is thus seen as having redemptive power for the person who undertakes it. Productivity has value beyond the external goods produced. Producing value also has worth in terms of the workers' experience of the world and their place in it.

We are created *b'tzelem Elohim,* in the image of the Creator. Our work is a manifestation of the Creator's creativity within us.   —S.P.W.

Those who can afford not to work should consider giving back to their communities by offering their services in areas of need, such as volunteer work, teaching and philanthropic pursuits. This applies equally to those who have retired and feel that they are due a rest based on their years of work. Even though one may feel entitled to be idle by virtual of earlier hard work and effort, it is important to reflect on the behavior one is modeling for others.   —M.N.

Volunteer work can be an important way to contribute to society and experience the dignity and honor that work affords. Participating in service projects or joining the board of a not-for-profit organization not only helps those who benefit from the volunteer's efforts. Often, volunteers report that they obtain great satisfaction and reward for what they give, though the currency is non-financial.   —M.K.

How do we define "work?" If someone is elderly, disabled, mentally challenged, or otherwise unable to be actively involved in the marketplace, and the action of working is fundamental and even redemptive, what might our society's obligation be to help such a person find meaningful work? *Avoda,* work, can also be defined as "sacred service," referring to religious and spiritual actions that do not involve *parnasa,* income-based work. Rather, *avoda* is effort extended to contribute to the spiritual economy. Perhaps we should consider *avoda* as a framework for thinking about meaningful work that can extend to all segments of the population. With that perspective, helping each person find ways to engage in some kind of *avoda* on a regular basis becomes a morally important action.   —M.K.

After eating the forbidden fruit, Adam was told that he would eat bread only by the sweat of his brow (Genesis 3:19), and the Talmud (*Pesaḥim* 118A) notes that he felt relieved upon hearing this because he understood that making bread involved toil that would separate him from the other animals. While work conveys dignity, idleness is often portrayed as dangerous. The Mishna (*Ketubot* 5.5) states that people who can afford not to work should work anyway because idleness can lead to lewdness or depression.

The rabbis say that no matter how wealthy one is, one has an obligation to personally play some role in the preparations for Shabbat. Without making the effort to prepare for Shabbat, we would not be able to fully appreciate the rest and joy that it brings. A midrash (*Tanḥuma Vayetze* 13) says that "when a person toils with both hands, God grants blessing." While we might not all agree with the the-

---

The punishments of Eden may also conceal blessings. Though work and childbirth may be among the most difficult of life's tasks, they can also be among the most rewarding. —D.E.

A great deal of leisure time can indeed be challenging, as witnessed by the difficulties sometimes encountered by those who retire after a lifetime of work. The loss of the structure of a job and the self-esteem that working usually generates can often have negative medical as well as emotional effects. —J.J.S.

The notion that work wards off lewdness or depression carries a certain irony in an era when we have become sensitized to issues such as sexual harassment on the job, the power inequities of most "office romances," and the numbing effect of certain kinds of repetitive "dead-end" jobs that offer only the promise of more of the same. —R.H.

Rashi suggests that when Shabbat comes, one must act *as if* all of one's work had been completed so that one can enter into rest deeply and completely. This can be a challenging mental and spiritual practice requiring discipline! But it points to an important teaching about healthy and balanced effort: When it is time to work, work! And when it is time to rest, rest fully both physically and mentally. Let go of thinking about work and the need to finish everything completely. There is an auspicious and dignified rhythm suggested between the balance of work and rest. —M.K.

ology of this passage, the point it makes about work is clear—our lives are shaped and given meaning, in part, by the work that we do.

Of course not all work conveys dignity. Oppressive work conditions, poor treatment of workers and devaluing the results of labor remove the meaning and satisfaction from work. Labor that is dehumanizing or degrading robs the worker of *kavod* (dignity or honor). Leading a life of *kavod* is one of the important reasons to work. Thus, a good society is one that ensures meaningful work to those who are willing and able to do it.

Work should not be understood in purely selfish terms as producing value only for the worker. One rabbinic tale (*Vayikra Rabba* 25.5) describes an old man planting a tree. The emperor Hadrian happens by and asks why the

---

One goal of the early Zionist revolution was to reinvigorate the spirit of the Jewish people through a return to physical labor. The writings of A.D. Gordon explore this theme in depth.   —D.E.

Marge Piercy, in the conclusion of her classic poem, "To Be of Use," helps us understand why work (*avoda*) equally connotes service and prayer: "The work of the world is common as mud. / Botched, it smears the hands, crumbles to dust. / But the thing worth doing well done / has a shape that satisfies, clean and evident. / Greek amphoras for wine or oil, / Hopi vases that held corn, are put in museums / but you know they were made to be used. / The pitcher cries for water to carry / and a person for work that is real."   —F.S.D.

As post-industrial society moves forward, many people experience their work as ungratifying, highly repetitive and poorly paying. But for many others there are increased opportunities for creative work. This is so not only for academicians, artists and craftspeople. It is also the case for many business executives, architects, physicians and countless others. For them work is a celebrated activity. How employers and employees can band together to enhance the opportunities for creative engagement becomes an ever more relevant question. It is critical to strengthening the spiritual aspect of work.   —D.A.T.

This popular story uses an apt metaphor. Our work is always about planting. We cannot know the final outcome. All we can do is labor with a clarity of wholesome intentions— plant seeds of *emet, kavod,* and *kehila* (truth, respect and community).   —S.P.W.

old man is planting the tree since it will take many years to bear fruit and the old man will not benefit. The old man replies that just as his ancestors planted for him, so is he planting for those who will come after him. Work can be a generative and redemptive act.

Employers must meet several conditions for work to produce *kavod* for their employees. The employer must treat the worker as a person who has *kavod*. The worker must see the work as accomplishing something worthwhile. And the conditions under which the worker labors must be compatible with worker dignity in terms of hours, expectations, safety, physical surroundings, compensation and so on. Those issues will be discussed further below.

The exploitation of workers in countries during the early stages of their industrialization is notorious. Globalization of the economy has helped to produce some of these abuses. It is also true, however, that globalization has operated through market forces to improve compensation in third-world countries, increase standards of worker and product safety, improve product quality and heighten environmental concern. Many Western businesses have, because of commercial pressures, taken increased responsibility for workers and the environment throughout their supply chains. Despite many ongoing abuses, this process has resulted in the gradual spread of ideas and best practices that have positively affected lives all over the globe. Those who encourage such corporate behavior are certainly engaged in *tikun olam,* the improvement of our world.   —N.P.

American governmental standards for workplace health are largely limited to physical well-being. By contrast, New Zealand's national agency for work welfare considers specific conditions that lead to psychological health at work.   —N.P.

One of the most consistent and central teachings of the biblical prophets was their profound objection to the exploitation of workers.   —T.K.

Obligations of Employers

Most forms of production and sales are more efficient when accomplished by a team of workers, and many of them cannot be done by one person working alone. As a result, most people work for someone else. This arrangement makes good economic sense, but it has many dangers because there is a striking imbalance between the power held by the employer and the power of the workers. This power imbalance has often allowed employers to treat workers in ways that violate their *kavod,* their dignity, because many employees are financially forced into employment situations where unfairly exploiting workers is a common practice.

The limits that *halakha* (Jewish law) could place on workers were themselves constrained by the fact that Jewish enterprises generally had to compete with similar enterprises owned by non-Jews. If the labor costs of the Jewish businesses were much greater than those of the non-Jewish ones, the Jewish enterprises would be forced out of business. The widespread use of technology and the advantages that stem from unique products and manufacturing methods have made the cost of labor less critical to the success of some business enterprises; however, the cost of labor is still a critical issue in competitiveness and profits in most enterprises. This is the main reason why so much labor-intensive manufacturing has moved to parts of the world where labor is less expensive. These issues

---

Jews have long championed the formation of labor unions and the collective bargaining process to equalize the power relationship of labor and capital. Jews have played a particularly active and influential role in the modern labor union movement.   —E.Z.

must be balanced against the ideal way in which workers should be treated. Causing businesses to fail unnecessarily not only unfairly deprives business owners, it also deprives employees of dignified work.

Because of these enduring issues, the rabbis spoke not so much about ideal employment conditions as about the minimum that could be expected. One such minimum was the right of an employee to use an outhouse when the need arose so that the person could have privacy and maintain dignity and comfort. Since such facilities were sometimes at a considerable distance from the workplace, this was a major time concession. The rabbis insisted upon this right because it is so essential to preserving the *kavod* of the individual. A full-time employee is similarly entitled to a reasonable amount of sick and personal leave, as well as vacation time, subject to negotiation and the terms of employment. Employee *kavod* also dictates that the workplace be free of harassment, including sexual harassment.

A second minimum condition was that compensation has to be at least comparable with the going rate. If it was the local custom for employers to provide lunch, for example, the Jewish employer was expected to provide a lunch of at least equal quality to the lunches that employers generally provided in that locale (Mishna *Bava Metzia* 7.1).

The right to bathroom breaks continues to be an issue in contemporary sweatshops despite the existence of indoor plumbing because ruthless employers want to maintain unbroken control over employees to maximize their output. —D.A.T.

An employer has the obligation to make employees' rights known explicitly as a further safeguard for maintaining the *kavod* of employees. For example, a person who is being sexually harassed may not know what mechanisms are available for protecting their rights to safety and dignity. An employer who makes such policies and procedures known to new employees helps to create an environment of *kavod* in the workplace. —M.K.

Compensation has to be paid immediately at the end of the pay period; a day laborer must be paid at the end of the day, while others by custom might be paid at the end of the week or the end of the month. The employer never has the right to delay the payment of wages (Leviticus 19:13).

A third minimum condition was that the employee's human needs should be taken into consideration. For example, an employee being paid by the number of pieces completed might by honest error break a few, resulting in costs that could be deducted from the employee's wages. If the employee were earning so little that the deduction would leave the employee without enough money to buy food, the employer should not deduct the costs from the wages, even if that is the usual custom (see B. Talmud, *Bava Metzia* 83a).

Fourth, employees are human beings who should not be treated like machines. Instructing, critiquing and super-

---

An employer may not have a right to withhold wages, but economic circumstances often intrude, such as when the employer herself has not been paid by those above her in order to produce the income needed to pay those in her employ.   —R.H.

Views of organizational life that developed during the Industrial Revolution confound the notion of the intrinsic worth of human beings. During the Machine Age, workers operating valuable equipment came to be considered as cogs in the system, not as persons with independent worth who have thoughts, feelings and aspirations.   —N.P.

If an employee is a good fit for the job, the tasks of instructing, critiquing and supervising the employee become a mutually valued form of teaching. Both the employer and employee can be enriched by the interaction. If the employee is not a good fit for the job, the same activities are likely to become burdensome to both parties.   —D.E.

It is often best to praise an employee publicly so that the behavior can be modeled to others. However, when critiquing an employee, it is always best to do it in private, even if the desire is to use the behavior as an educational opportunity for others. *Kavod* also suggests that employees be given an opportunity to evaluate their individual performances in light of their personal assessments of their strengths, weaknesses and areas for personal growth. Concern for *kavod* also includes matching individuals to employment opportunities that best fit their own understanding of their strengths and weaknesses.   —M.N.

vising are often necessary business activities. They should be undertaken in ways that do not damage the *kavod* of the employee. Employees are also entitled to have clear job descriptions, regular evaluations that are performed in an honest, caring way, and promotions that reflect performance and capability.

Fifth, since employers establish the terms and conditions of work, they must take reasonable precautions to provide for the safety of employees. Employers' ability to provide for workplace safety is greater than that of their employees, so employers bear moral responsibility for accidents that they could have prevented. The precautions for which employers are responsible include maintaining facilities, machinery and tools in good repair; minimizing exposure to toxic substances; and providing safety training. Where possible, hazards to health and safety should be removed. Where that is not possible, all reasonable precautions should be taken. Proper lighting, heat and air conditioning appropriate to the nature of the workplace are also health and safety issues.

Contemporary Jewish employers have a minimum obligation to provide the prevailing compensation—salary and benefits—to their employees. If employers were required to pay significantly more than the prevailing rate, that might result in their being unable to compete in the marketplace.

Finding the "prevailing rate" for certain forms of employment is a challenging and often ephemeral task. Synagogues frequently search for the prevailing rate for rabbinic compensation through taking surveys or referring to median or averaged salaries, without taking into account the variables of, for example, cost of living and price of housing. Translating rabbinic experience and ability into economic terms becomes particularly problematic when one synagogue calls another to ask how much the rabbi gets paid—without always considering, for example, the size of the congregation, or a disparity in years of experience between two rabbis.   —R.H.

Therefore the prevailing rate is a sound minimum, but employers can of course compensate at a higher rate if they choose. In the United States, where the prevailing compensation by custom includes health insurance, the employer has an obligation to provide a reasonable level of health insurance until such time as that benefit is provided by the government. Similarly, employers have an obligation to follow prevailing custom by making Social Security payments (which of course are also a legal requirement), providing pensions and offering salaries that constitute a living wage. The failure of some employers to do so does not justify violating the more ethical prevailing custom.

When does enlightened behavior become paternalism? Rather than provide the same benefits for all employees regardless of their personal situation, many large, American companies today provide a cafeteria plan for benefits, at a cost of between 18 percent and 25 percent of base compensation. Respecting the diversity of the workforce, these plans permit each employee to decide how to allocate benefit dollars: health insurance, dental and vision care, additional retirement funding, life and disability insurance, educational funding for themselves or their children, or additional compensation. Such plans provide the organization with a flexible means to address all of their employees' needs without being discriminatory, while at the same time controlling the cost per employee. —M.N.

If it is indeed a requirement for Jewish employers to pay a living wage, this would make many companies non-competitive in the American economy in many cities. In many areas, living wage is two to three times the minimum wage. On a policy level, Jews should support efforts to raise the minimum wage and to index it to inflation, so that a living wage level becomes institutionalized. —A.A.

When Adat Shalom moved into its new building in Bethesda, Maryland, in 2001, we were dismayed at how little groundskeepers were paid. We ended up paying our janitorial services company several thousands of dollars *above* their bid so that all our employees could receive a livable wage with health benefits. A beloved janitor, himself a South American immigrant working hard and well in order to send money back home, later came down with acute appendicitis; only because he had insurance was it caught early. What price should we have placed on his life or on our culpability, had we not gone the "extra mile?" —F.S.D.

Companies that create work situations well suited to working mothers are current exemplars of *menschlich* treatment of workers. Paradoxically, the altruistic motive proves to make good business sense, as companies with such policies attract and retain employees with a good work ethic. —N.P.

A few years ago a Jew who owned a small firm that manufactured lamps argued that applying these standards would drive him out of business because all his competitors ran sweatshops. Since Jews are obliged to follow the laws of the country where they are located (*dina d' malkhuta dina*) as long as those laws are not unethical, it was pointed out that he had no right to earn a living that way. Changing his practice while providing information on his competitors to the government might well make him a hero, and his business might improve because of increased employee and customer loyalty. "In a place where there is no *mensch*, be a *mensch*" (*Pirkey Avot* 2.6). But even if his business might fail because he did the right thing, running an illegal sweatshop is not an ethically acceptable option. Nevertheless, it might happen that an owner who lived in a place where sweatshop conditions were legal paid marginally better wages and provided slightly better working conditions than the competition; if the employees could not find better jobs if the owner weren't operating, then the owner's decision about

Today the "minimum wage" is better described and understood as a "living wage." An employee's salary should, in the best case scenario, support a full *life* for the employee.
—Y.R.

Kavod is intangible; minimum wage is concrete. Yet there is no *kavod* without a decent living. These two are as inseparable as heaven and earth, Creator and created, thought, word and deed. This is Jewish embodiment, Jewish incarnation.   —S.P.W.

American Jews who are descended from those who arrived from Eastern Europe during the 1881–1924 wave of immigration share a familial memory of what it means to be an oppressed laborer. Just as the Torah is clear that the Israelites should not oppress the stranger because we were strangers in the land of Egypt, so does the progressive impulse of many of us derive from empathy generated by the stories of our immigrant parents and grandparents. Our challenge is to remain empathic because of our values, even when we no longer directly identify with oppressed laborers.   —J.J.S.

whether to run such a shop would be a difficult one. The general rule is that an employer cannot be expected to go very far beyond the standards of the market in which the owner operates.

One of the reasons Jews have generally supported laws that raise the minimum wage is that preserving *kavod* requires earning a sufficient living to provide food, shelter, clothing and medical care. It is extraordinarily difficult to live with *kavod* when earning the minimum wage in many countries. When the salary floor is raised, the entire scale of salaries is eventually affected. From a Jewish perspective, that is a good thing.

Some employers pay their employees entirely or partly in cash with the unspoken understanding that they will not declare some or all of their wages for the purpose of paying taxes. This saves the employer from paying into a retirement plan (such as Social Security in the United States), for unemployment insurance and perhaps for other payments. In the short run, this also saves the employee money. However, this practice has other effects that are pernicious. It prevents the employee from collecting unemployment insurance and from receiving Social Security or other retirement benefits, and this may also

There are many gray areas that fall between the illegal and the unethical. For example, on a close call an employer might categorize an employee as "self-employed" (IRS 1099 vs. IRS W2) in order to avoid paying the half of the Social Security tax incumbent upon employers. This leaves the "self-employed" person responsible for the entire amount. Under a narrow interpretation of the statute, the employer could be right, but if by an equally legitimate reading of IRS regulations, the person could be classified as an employee and the employer refuses to do so, this surely raises an issue of ethics.   —R.H.

Some employers increasingly seem to be defining positions just short enough of "full time" to avoid an obligation to pay benefits received by full-time employees.   —R.H.

have a broader social cost if, as a result, the employee becomes a ward of the state. Not paying taxes also throws an unfair burden on those who do pay taxes and encourages a breakdown of trust in the tax-collection system. This conduct on the part of employers is illegal (and therefore a violation of *dina d'malkhuta dina*) and unethical. An individual or family that pays a full-time nanny or housekeeper in cash is in the same category.

More complicated is the situation in which a household worker such as a cleaner or babysitter works part-time and has many clients. That person can be perceived as running a small business rather than functioning as an employee, in which case the business—even though it has a sole proprietor—is liable for taxes and benefits. When the worker says that this is the case, there is an obligation to follow the definitions in local law (*dina d'malkhuta dina*).

When a potential employee is an undocumented worker who cannot legally work locally and therefore cannot pay employment-related taxes, it is generally improper to hire that person. One exception occurs when hiring such a

---

If one engages an undocumented alien for work, one should be particularly careful to deal very fairly with that worker. Taking advantage of that person's circumstances is egregious *ona'a*. The presence of undocumented workers in the United States is so pervasive (and has been tolerated by the federal government for so long) that at times it may be impractical to avoid dealing with them.   —L.S.

It is possible to view the nation's immigration policies as grossly unjust on a large scale, so that employing an undocumented worker can be an act of conscientious objection, an act of observing the biblical commandment to protect the *ger*, the resident alien, when civil law has declared that mitzvah to be illegal. People usually come to the U.S. to earn a living wage because they cannot do so in their countries of origin. For those who believe that American foreign-trade policies exacerbate this problem while increasing domestic profits, there is even less motivation to respect these laws. In such a complicated situation, it does not necessarily make sense to invoke the principle of *dina d'malkhuta dina*.   —J.J.S.

worker is an act of conscientious objection. This unusual circumstance might occur if the employer believed that the potential employee was being unfairly treated by the government that was withholding asylum, and that sending that employee back to the employee's home country would put the employee or a member of the employee's family in danger. Generally the potential employee's friendship, desire for economic success or usefulness as an employee does not legitimate violating the law.

Employers often enter into formal agreements or contracts with employees. When they do so, employers are morally bound by the terms of the contract, but employees can leave before the term of the contract is up. Allowing an employee to leave before the contract is up provides a way to address the power imbalance between employer and employee. It allows the employee to leave an abusive employer or one who is underpaying or one who provides

Conscientious objection may indeed be called for in the face of tightening immigration laws, xenophobic popular sentiment, and the Kafkaesque challenges facing even legal immigrants. At minimum, our values and our history call us to help reform and liberalize America's immigration laws. We must not let Lady Liberty's lamp be lowered, nor allow the closing of Emma Lazarus's "golden door."   —F.S.D.

Congregations are sometimes upset when negotiations with a prospective rabbi are not successfully concluded: "But you already accepted the position!" It is crucial to frame an initial invitation for rabbinic employment as "We are inviting you into negotiations in the hope that they will conclude successfully and you will become our rabbi."   —R.H.

Many companies that need to protect trade secrets insert a "non-compete" clause in employee contracts. This clause prevents employees from going to work for a competitor immediately after leaving their employers, thereby reducing the risk of their improperly using information that they may have gleaned from their previous workplace. This clause protects employers from possible theft of clients or information, and therefore is not an unfair restriction on employee mobility. It is unethical to conduct industrial espionage in any form in order to obtain the proprietary information of a competitor.   —M.N.

insufficient opportunities for advancement. It allows the employee to accept a better-paying, more prestigious, or otherwise preferable job. If an employee is forced by financial pressure to accept a long-term contract and then must pass up other economic opportunities, this amounts to improper coercion. Invalidating such coercion is in the interest of preventing the employee from experiencing involuntary servitude (*issur shibud haguf*).

Allowing the employee to leave before the end of the contract thus avoids several potential evils. However, the employee is not allowed to leave the employer at the beginning of a busy season when the employee cannot be replaced. For a farm worker, this would mean not departing during the harvest season; for a store employee, it might mean not leaving during the Christmas rush. For a rabbi, it might mean not announcing a departure so close to the High Holy Days that the congregation could not arrange for a suitable replacement. Sometimes professional associations provide stricter guidelines. One is ethically bound to follow the rules of an association of which one is a member.

The nature of rabbinic contracts is a frequent source of controversy and conflict. Congregations often assume that a rabbi has no right—legal, ethical or professional—to leave employment prior to the end of a contract (a right assumed and usually exercised by almost every member of a synagogue board in their own employment). Rather than seeing a contract as protection for the rabbi, congregations often see it as an instrument of control. Rabbinic contracts ought to carry a clause outlining procedures for early termination that offer a congregation a reasonable amount of notification time in order to hire another rabbi, while preserving the right of the incumbent rabbi to seek or accept another position prior to the end of a contract. The Reconstructionist movement's report on rabbi-congregation relations explicitly states that "Because of the power and economic imbalance between the rabbi as employee and the congregation as employer, contracts primarily protect the rabbi, not the congregation."   —R.H.

Allowing an employee to leave during a contract is a direct outgrowth of understanding *avadim hayinu b'mitzrayim*—ongoing empathy with the least powerful.   —S.P.W.

What constitutes a fair wage? In Jewish tradition, there was no limit on what an owner could earn as long as the profit made on selling any particular item did not involve too high a markup. The kinds of wealth that have been accumulated in recent generations, however, are without parallel. The traditional Jewish response to the accumulation of great wealth was to recognize the right of individuals to accumulate and enjoy such wealth but at the same time to increase the community's expectation of how much money and time the wealthy would make available to meet communal needs and, in some cases, to formalize that through taxation.

The accumulation of wealth has traditionally not had a moral cap as long as the wealth was accumulated by ethical means. Similarly there has been no cap on salaries and other compensation paid to employees. The situation of differentiated earnings based on knowledge, skill and

In congregational life, it is customary for wealthier members to contribute more—either into an operating fund or into special funds for projects that need extraordinary funding. This illustrates "from each according to her ability" in practice.   —N.P.

In my view, the Jewish approach of balancing fairness and consequences supports state intervention to address the issue of the excessive accumulation of wealth. The strict consequentialist may dismiss any concern over such inequities on the grounds that it is a result of an efficient market mechanism that maximizes overall wealth and thus "raises all boats," but it is a specious argument that a more graduated tax structure would discourage individual initiative at the upper margin. The moral imperative to create a more just society, which presumes such benefits as universal health care and a living wage for everyone in the work force, trumps the libertarian aversion to virtually any state-mandated redistribution of wealth. As this *Guide* indicates, Jewish ethical tradition supports this view.   —J.N.C.

experience has always existed, but in recent years the range of salaries in some developed countries has grown ever wider. Top executives earn at least 20 times the wage of the lowest-paid full-time employee, and some of them earn as much as 400 times the lowest wage. This may not raise questions about how much the highest-paid employee may earn, but it raises substantial questions of unfairness if the lowest-paid employee earns too little to live a life that has *kavod*. When that is the case, it is an ethical failure that begs for corporate attention. When corporate boards and senior employees work together to raise their compensation, it also strongly raises the ethical question as to whether they are properly fulfilling their fiduciary responsibility as stewards of the corporation's resources and overseers of the stockholders' return on investment.

The question of absolute versus relative economic well-being should not be sidestepped. A society in which some people are earning far more than others is not problematical if the people earning less have sufficient income to live in a dignified way with all their basic needs met. True, many people would rather be relatively well-off than absolutely well-off. Survey evidence is mixed on this issue. But surely it can be argued that people who are concerned less by their own living standard than by whether they are "keeping up with the Joneses" are not doing their children any favor. Indeed, they may be violating the "do not covet" value of Judaism.   —E.Z.

Recent developments in socially responsible corporate compensation cap senior executive compensation at seven times the pay of the lowest-paid employee. However, it is unusual for publicly held corporations to adopt this statute.   —N.P.

In 1962, the wealth of the richest one percent of U.S. households was roughly 125 times greater than that of the typical household. By 2004, it was 190 times (Economic Policy Institute, *State of Working America 2006–07*). The Torah provided a radical wealth redistribution model in the Jubilee and the *sh'mita*. Even if these practices were never observed, I believe the Torah is telling us that huge variations in wealth are not what God intended for Israel. What does this mean for us today?   —A.A.

When employment contracts are being negotiated, deceptive practices ought to be avoided. Since bluffing is deceptive, it is also improper. The principle of *hin tzedek*, good-faith negotiation, applies here as well. The goal is to arrive at a contract that will be favorable to both sides through a process characterized by *hin tzedek*. Honest disclosure of facts and perspectives plays an important role in such a process.

Obligations of Employees

The most basic obligation of an employee is to work for the benefit of the employer. The employee has an obligation to come to work well-rested, sober, on time and appropriately attired. While employees are entitled to sufficient breaks to eat, relieve themselves and make brief phone calls to stay in touch with family and friends, this should be in the context of using their best efforts to fulfill their job responsibilities. Regardless of how the employees feel about the employer, they must do their best work as

---

Deuteronomy 6:18, "Do what is right and good in the sight of God," is the basis for the State of Israel Contracts Law of 1973. Section 12(a) states, "Contract negotiations must be conducted in the usual and customary manner and in good faith." Section 39 says, "A contractual obligation shall be performed and a right arising out of a contract shall be exercised in the usual and customary manner and in good faith."   —L.K.

Sustainability and sustainable investing are relatively new managerial concepts that involve evaluating an organization's business practices not in terms of current profitability, but rather in terms of their long-term sustainability of profits. Sustainability from a business perspective includes nourishing a skilled workforce, interacting appropriately with the community and the environment, and treating clients in ways that develop long-term relationships. Studies have shown that following sustainable business practices can lead to higher, long-term stakeholder returns.   —M.N.

long as they stay employed. The employees' efforts should carry out the wishes and serve the best interests of their employer as long as those interests and wishes do not conflict with standards of ethical behavior or with any applicable law. If there is such a conflict, the employees' first obligation is to act ethically and legally.

If an employee chooses to retire or to change employers, the employee has an obligation to provide reasonable notice so that the employer can prepare for the change. That notice would necessarily be longer during a peak business period than when there is less work to be done. It would also be longer for a more highly paid, more senior employee. Often the amount of notice is arrived at by mutual agreement. The employee has no obligation to stay until a search for a replacement has been conducted nor to fulfill the length of time on a contract, but does have an obligation not to leave at peak season or in the middle of a short but important project.

An employee has an obligation not to disparage an employer in a way that damages the employer's reputation or business unless doing so involves *azhara,* warning, or *tokheḥa,* reproof (see those parts in the *Ethics of*

Beyond the very basic obligation of honest work for honest pay, an employee owes the enterprise a duty of loyalty. Becoming a participant in the achievement of the enterprise's goals is part of how an employee achieves *kavod* and self-fulfillment. In public companies, practically everyone is an employee, and the owners (shareholders) act through the board of directors. In successful companies, almost everyone, from the top management to the most humble employees, embraces common goals and seeks self-realization by doing well for the enterprise. The level of this personal engagement may be the most important difference between a first-rate and a mediocre enterprise.   —L.S.

Speech section of *A Guide to Jewish Practice*). The obligation not to disparage one's employer applies both while the employee is employed and after the employment ends. The employee also has an obligation to safeguard any proprietary information that the employer has. The employee must not utilize that information or share it with anyone else without the employer's explicit permission. This is the case both during the period of employment and after it ends. Taking proprietary information or using it without permission is a form of theft. A former employee opening a competitive business can use the skills learned from the former employer but must carefully avoid using proprietary information.

Employees can negotiate their compensation individually, but they also have the right to address the natural power imbalance between employers and employees by joining together and bargaining collectively. Employees have the right to unionize (based on B. Talmud, *Bava Batra* 8b–9a and the commentary on it by the Rosh; this is also the understanding of the 20th century scholar of *halakha* Moshe Feinstein). If bargaining fails to produce a mutually acceptable result and fair arbitration is unavailable, employees also have the right to strike. Employers have the right to lock out employees if the two sides can-

---

The placement guidelines of the Reconstructionist movement specifically state that a congregation may negotiate with only one rabbi at a time, and that a rabbi may negotiate with only one congregation at a time. Parallel negotiations in the hope of "getting the best deal" are demeaning to both parties.   —R.H.

When opening contract negotiations with a rabbi, a congregation should present an appropriate compensation package. A negotiator should not first ask a rabbi, "What are your salary expectations?"   —R.H.

not come to terms. Neither side has the right to use phys-ical force against the other, since such violence is forbid-den in general. Both sides are forbidden to retaliate against those who organize or who speak out for positions with which they disagree. When such strikes and lockouts will damage the community, the community has the right to intervene and provide mediation and, where law per-mits, require arbitration. Attaining fair negotiations, ensuring sufficient employee compensation, having busi-nesses that thrive and living in a harmonious community are all legitimate concerns of the community as a whole.

Employees and employers separately or jointly can also work together for broader social change in such areas as med-ical insurance, minimum wage standards, unemployment insurance, the banning of unscrupulous business practices and other matters of concern that are best dealt with on a broader level than that of a single business. Such change may

Sometimes when an employee takes a stand for ethical standards or against legal infrac-tions, it can put that person's job security at risk. Whistleblowers rarely find a receptive environment for their efforts. Thus it can require great courage to confront wrongdo-ing. It can likewise require courage and sacrifice for an employer to respond to an employee's concerns with integrity and reparative action. Such courage is a fundamen-tal component of maintaining healthy organizational ethics.   —M.K.

Some rabbis choose to have a representative negotiate their contract with a congregation rather than engage in a give-and-take that can intrude on the rabbi-congregation rela-tionship.   —R.H.

The centrality of American Jews in the early labor movement can hardly be overstated—from the masses of the "uprising of the 20,000" and the International Ladies' Garment Workers Union to thoughtful pot-stirrers like Emma Goldman, big shots like Samuel Gompers, and martyrs like the victims of the 1911 Triangle Shirtwaist Factory fire. The union story is our story, whether it is about Moses organizing Bricklayers Local 1 in Goshen or today's domestic workers and day laborers struggling for justice.   —F.S.D.

be pursued through creating industry standards, passing new legislation, pursuing court decisions and other methods.

Competition and Cooperation

The primarily agricultural economy described in the Torah and the more urban economy that existed in the rabbinic period were both characterized by the trading of goods, existence of craftspeople and private ownership of property. There was a market economy. The Torah insisted on honest weights and measures, and the rabbis in that context expanded on this principle to insist on disclosure of any flaws in the goods being sold. Their effort to create the safest possible environment for buyers often rested on the biblical principle that one may not put a stumbling block before the blind (Leviticus 19:14). Without full disclosure, they argued, the buyer is unable to fully see the product and could stumble in making a decision as to whether to purchase.

Marketplaces—whether temporary stands in a small village or stores in large suburban malls or Internet websites—succeed when they are an effective and reasonably efficient means for the distribution of goods. The nature of market-

The Fourteenth Amendment to the U.S. Constitution, ratified in 1868, was initially all about *tzelem Elohim* (the dignity of being created in the Divine Image) because it enfranchised former slaves and other minority individuals and provided "equal protection" to all. Its "due-process" clause was heralded as a progressive innovation. But for the past century, the overwhelming majority of Fourteenth Amendment cases have focused on treating corporations as individuals with rights, with due process employed to invalidate a wide range of social regulation. American law, like society, has far to go if it is to return to its putative focus on dignity and equality. —F.S.D.

Forbidding the use of stumbling blocks is in direct opposition to many tactics of the contemporary advertising industry. Advertising often depends on our weaker sides (our blindness)—the need for approval, conformity, quick fixes and the eroticized desire for the next thing. It feeds a mistaken notion of what leads to true happiness. —S.P.W.

places is that the prices and quality of goods are determined by competition. For the marketplace to function with maximal efficiency, buyers need to know their choices in terms of prices and the nature of the goods available. Greater efficiency is achieved when buyers and sellers cooperate to share non-proprietary information as thoroughly as possible. Posting prices at the booths in a vegetable market or detailed descriptions of houses for sale on real estate brokerage websites, for example, helps in the fair and efficient distribution of goods. Disclosing pre-existing conditions to a medical insurer keeps insurance rates lower for everyone else. For competition to be effective, a considerable level of cooperation is needed among buyers and sellers, consumers and producers. This is true whether someone is hiring an employee, buying grapes, selecting a physician, or negotiating with a contractor about the building of a house.

Cooperation has other advantages as well. Since those who do business together tend to deal with each other repeatedly, developing trust is advantageous. It saves time, makes interactions more pleasant, and allows people to maintain a positive frame of mind toward others rather than focus on guarding against potential exploitation. When the people with whom one does business are also neighbors, friends or colleagues in communal endeavors, trust and mutual concern in the business realm help to generate positive relationships in these other spheres of life.

Market-based competition is a pricing method intended to maximize profits rather than generate a fair price. Socially responsible companies use other approaches to pricing that are designed to charge a price that produces enough profit to sustain the company, but not so much as to take advantage of the unknown buyers.   —N.P.

Because of the potential for conflict, hurt feelings, and associated employment problems (including role confusion and perceptions of compromised confidentiality), many synagogues wisely adopt a policy of not hiring congregants for staff positions.   —R.H.

When people conduct business based on exploitative efforts to seek any possible advantage over others, the suspicion and animosity generated create friction and inefficiency in business relationships. The corrosion of character involved also affects the inner lives of the individuals, and often their other relationships. The rabbis wanted to avoid that because they were concerned with character development and with creating communities focused on higher values. They suggested that a good transaction is one where both sides benefit. That description implies that it is incumbent upon the people on each side in a business transaction to ensure that it benefits not only themselves, but the other people with whom they are interacting.

While spending an under-financed post-college year in Israel, I couldn't believe the chutzpah of the elderly Jews who would sit at the entrance to public bathrooms, asking for 20 *agurot* (a nickel or dime). Based on a poverty mindset and a misguided understanding of public facilities, I refused to pay, which sometimes occasioned sharp words. Only later did I guiltily realize that they were not *schnorrers* (panhandlers), but struggling folks who took it upon themselves to clean public places that would not have been cleaned otherwise—and whom the community supported, if minimally, for their efforts. Only later still did I guiltily realize that there is dignity to being a *schnorrer,* and *schnorrers* deserve our support. —F.S.D.

The goal of mutual benefit is holistic or covenantal. It valorizes process and relationship above outcome, product and profit. —S.P.W.

To ensure that a business transaction benefits both parties involved, it behooves each party to consider the contract between them as a *brit*—a covenant. From the employer's perspective, the transaction requires attention and intention. From the employee's perspective, the transaction requires awareness and understanding. When each party can recognize the needs of the other and acknowledge individual responsibility to ensure the terms of the agreement, then the qualities of a sacred relationship can be readily experienced. —Y.R.

It is common for negotiators to seek a transaction where both sides benefit, and to refer to it as a "win-win" transaction. *Getting to Yes,* a popular book about business negotiation, suggests that a win-win approach is the most effective in business dealings. —L.S./N.P.

When everybody benefits, that's good business. The goal of business should not be solely to maximize profit. It should be to make the largest profit possible while accomplishing other critical goals, such as maintaining the integrity of the marketplace, ensuring that people are treated with *kavod,* and strengthening the community within which the transactions take place. A similar approach to business ethics can be found in stakeholder theory, an increasingly popular approach to management explored in a substantial body of literature written by economists and business theorists. Stakeholder theory recognizes that business enterprises affect many people—not only owners and workers, but also suppliers, customers and everyone affected by the economic relationships generated and by the environmental and communal impact of the business. Ethical business approaches must weigh the full impact of the business on all its stakeholders.

It is correct that Jewish ethics does not condone profit maximization as the sole goal of business. There are, indeed, other valid stakeholders. But within an overall framework of multiple stakeholders, profit maximization is not a Jewishly unethical goal.   —E.Z.

The attempt to broaden corporate management responsibilities to go beyond shareholders to some broader, more ambiguous set of "stakeholders" may be more consistent with Jewish ethical principles, and it can be urged upon corporations, but it is unlikely to find its way into American law because that would require a total overhaul of the legal concept of fiduciary responsibility. That is a virtually impossible task in my view, given the inherent ambiguities and potential disagreement as to what constitutes a "stakeholder." How could we determine the proper hierarchy of stakeholders from a quantitative point of view, particularly if the class of stakeholders is broadened to go beyond shareholders and employees of a corporation? In addressing issues of corporate polluting and overall use of scarce resources, the class of relevant stakeholders can arguably be the entire planet.   —J.N.C.

Contemporary Jews live far from the world of the *shtetl*. Many people are engaged in enterprises that span huge distances, and many business transactions are between people who do not have significant social relationships. Do attitudes and practices that grew up in a more localized, community context apply equally well in our world? One of the principles that the rabbis asserted (based on Leviticus 24:22 and Exodus 12:49) is that non-Jews should be treated with the same ethical consideration with which Jews are treated. This demand indicates that the rabbis understood the issue of a broader context. In fact for the last 2,000 years, many Jews have done business primarily with non-Jews, and many of them did business in disparate geographic locations. This is not a new phenomenon. Concern with character and relationships transcends time and space.

Many of the laws governing the marketplace found in the Talmud (especially in *Bava Metzia*) specifically stipulate behavior expected when dealing with non-Jews. —N.H.M.

Exodus 12:49 teaches that there should be *torah achat,* one teaching, one set of laws that should guide both citizen and stranger alike. Individuals were not to be judged on their origin, but as participating members of the larger community. As American Jews we live in two civilizations simultaneously—the Jewish and the American. As a result, the ways in which we move back and forth between these worlds demands that we not discriminate and that we engage in a global marketplace regardless of religious background. —Y.R.

Many corporate executives note that their companies' largest suppliers and customers have done business together for several decades. They trust each other and look out for each other not primarily because of abstract principles of ethics but because it is good business practice. They cooperate for each other's mutual benefit. @T: A corporation had a multiyear contract for raw materials with one of its suppliers. The supplier was caught by surprise during a rapid rise in the cost of raw goods and would have been bankrupted if the corporation had insisted that the contract be honored. The corporation instead renegotiated the contract. This generated loyalty, ensured the continued capacity of the supplier to serve the corporation, and preserved valued business relationships. Often moral principles and self-interest go hand-in-hand. When they conflict, principles should come first, but if the result

In the financial markets, your word is your bond. Transactions of millions and even billions of dollars are executed based on verbal communications between individuals who rely on their reputation for honest dealing. Disagreements are resolved using time-honored methods—and a reputation that has been tarnished or even questioned is not easily restored. In the interest of expediency, a buyer or seller often takes a "short cut" and gains an unfair advantage, either intentionally or unintentionally. As a consistent practice, this can have long-term, negative effects. "Fool me once, shame on you; fool me twice, shame on me." A good name has value.   —M.N.

would be disastrous on a personal level, it's time to consider switching to a different business.

The Seller's Obligations

In light of the desire to promote honesty and cooperation and to ensure that both parties to a transaction benefit, sellers have many constraints placed upon them (Leviticus 25:14). The examples from Jewish ethics that follow should be understood as a representative sampling rather than an exhaustive list of contemporary moral concerns raised by sales.

If a seller has announced a price, the seller is obligated to sell at that price; the seller may not renege. When presenting goods for sale, the seller must display them in a way that gives an accurate picture of what is being sold, and of course the weight or quantity must be accurately stated. All flaws in the goods being sold must be clearly disclosed (the 12th century scholar Rambam, *Mishneh Torah, Hilkhot Meḥira* 15.6); goods with flaws can be sold as long as the flaws have been disclosed in advance. A basket of peaches, for example, must be arranged so that the bad ones aren't at the bottom of the basket and the best ones displayed. When a merchant sells a mixed-nut concoction, the nuts on top must be a fair representation of the nature of the mix. Accurate descriptions are critically important when buying goods via phone or the Internet.

The commitment to disclosing flaws honestly is antithetical to the airbrushing of reality that is routine in advertising.   —S.P.W.

Used goods must not be polished or packaged in a way that suggests that they are new (*Shulḥan Arukh, Ḥoshen Mishpat* 228.9). If goods are mixed, the seller must disclose the nature of the blend. This principle applies, for example, when there are several kinds of wine in a bottle or several sources of grain in a bin. Packaging should not create the illusion that more is in the package than is actually there. Many of the relatively recent American regulations regarding food and drugs are similar to these principles, though the Jewish approach covers raw goods far more extensively. In this regard, ethics can cover more than law, as contemporary marketing techniques clearly demonstrate—compliance with the law does not eliminate the opportunity to deceive through the way that goods are packaged.

One of the issues of marketplace ethics is what is allowed in attempting to attract buyers. Advertising the price and features of products is a legitimate way to attract customers; advertising that deceives in any way is not legitimate—see the section on "Truth, Lies and Advertising" in the *Ethics of Speech* section of *A Guide to Jewish Practice.*

Contemporary corporations often seriously violate the principle of honest packaging and maintaining quality. The seats on airplanes keep getting smaller. Have you noticed how small the macaroons are in the Passover tins? The weight goes down, but the can looks the same.   —S.P.W.

The nature of the advertising industry is to attempt to create demand where none existed, an approach that raises serious ethical concerns. The oversimplifications and half-truths common in advertising are bad enough, but worse still are the perceived needs or desires that ads are designed to instill in us. The environmental and social impact of unneeded purchases is huge, as is the subtle but real psychic damage of being repeatedly told that our choices or realities or possibilities simply don't measure up.   —F.S.D.

Using loss-leaders (products sold at a price below cost to attract buyers who will purchase other products at the same time) is a legitimate way to attract customers. Inaccurately describing products or advertising products that are not available is not. According to the rabbis, merchants are not allowed to lure minors who are running errands for their parents by offering them sweets because this may result in the minors, who are functioning as agents, not doing the best job possible for their parents. If the sweets are given when the minors would be buying there anyway, that is ethical because people should be able to do things that give pleasure to other members of the community (Mishna, *Bava Metzia* 4.12).

It is important for a seller to ask a buyer about the purpose of the purchase because the seller should guard against selling goods for a purpose that the goods cannot accom-

This, I believe, is a significant exception to the assumption of arms-length dealing where buyers are expected to look out for their own interest because minors are not deemed capable of doing due diligence. Misleading advertising to minors is one of the most serious ethical violations in which businesses regularly engage.   —E.Z.

Our obligations to minors have profound obligations for fast-food companies, which intentionally and aggressively advertise sugary, high-fat products to children.   —N.P.

I would agree that the long-run viability of a business is helped by keeping the buyer's interest front and center, but Jewish ethics does not always require this. Traditional Jewish business ethics presupposes a marketplace of arms-length dealing between sellers and buyers of most products and services (other than consulting services, where sellers do have a fiduciary responsibility). Deliberate deception, by either the seller or the buyer, is forbidden. But, within the bounds of honest dealing, both parties must engage in due diligence as each acts in his/her own self-interest.   —E.Z.

plish. This means that a hardware store, for example, should not sell non-galvanized nails (since they will rust) for shingling a roof, and that dry-clean-only fabric should not be sold to someone who wants to make beachwear. Stores selling high-tech products often have employees or owners with much more knowledge of the goods and their capacities, limits and alternatives than many buyers have, so they have a particular obligation to ensure that their customers make appropriate selections, neither buying more than is appropriate nor buying equipment that is insufficiently durable. The seller has a relationship to the buyer and should attempt to act in the buyer's interest by helping the buyer select appropriate goods. If the seller does not have appropriate goods for the buyer's purpose, the seller is obligated to disclose this. The seller's obligation to look out for the buyer's interest also applies to whether the seller should recommend add-ons, such as extended-coverage service contracts and peripheral equipment.

While the seller has an obligation to provide information useful to the buyer, the seller is not required to provide propriety information, such as a valuable formula or process developed by the seller for manufacturing. The seller also has no obligation to disclose when a subsequent shipment of goods will arrive if that will affect the seller's price, or how much the seller paid for the goods. Thus the seller is allowed to be self-protective and to maintain a competitive advantage over competitors as long as the seller also helps the buyer to make the best possible decisions within those constraints. The integrity of the transaction depends upon the delicate balancing of competition with cooperation.

The seller is limited to making a reasonable profit on goods. The rabbis intervened when price gouging took place (Mishna, *K'ritot* 1.7). Price gouging and fraud are forms of *ona'a* (oppression). When a seller accidentally overcharges a buyer, the seller should make up the difference as soon as the error is pointed out. If the seller intentionally charged more than a small percentage above what other sellers were charging in the same vicinity for the same goods, then that seller has done something unethical, and the seller has an obligation to make it up to the buyer (see Mishna, *Bava Metzia* 4.3–4). But overcharging is only for comparable goods at the same time in the same market. Goods sold just before a new supply becomes available will be more expensive than they will be later, so it is not reasonable to expect the prices to remain stable.

An extraordinarily efficient seller can drive other sellers out of a market by establishing selling prices below the costs of competitors. Sometimes this is achieved by economies of scale and sometimes by the use of new technology. These changes are often beneficial to the common good in the long run, but in the short run they can cause considerable damage through the loss of livelihoods and of dignity, as well as through bankruptcies. Where the prod-

Reasonable profit in my opinion is not an actionable concept because there is enormous room for differences of opinion about what is reasonable. Surely the rabbinic one-third markup over cost is arbitrary and takes no account of differences in risk undertaken in one business compared with another. That is why "profit maximization" is a legitimate goal—as long as the interests of other stakeholders are also respected.   —E.Z.

The overpricing of oil on several occasions in the United States resulted in federal and state investigations without any refund or restitution ever being ordered by the government or offered by the oil companies. Their actions would have had to be different if they had adopted the policy that restitution is required in the case of substantial overpricing.   —N.P.

ucts themselves remain unchanged—as is usually the case with big-box stores and increased uses of computerization in manufacturing—some Jewish traditions suggest that the price changes ought to be introduced slowly so that the impact on affected individuals and on the community can be absorbed at a rate that is less destructive. However, in our current economic situation this contradicts the principle of avoiding excessive profits because the company lowering the price slowly would be making far too much money during the period of change. To minimize the difficulties of economic dislocation, intervention in the form of retraining, job placement and short-term financial support should be seen as a communal responsibility.

When someone is selling land (which might or might not have a house or commercial building on it) that person has an obligation to offer it to the owner(s) of adjacent property because they might be interested in owning land adjacent to their own (B. Talmud *Bava Metzia* 108a-b). As long as they buy at the market rate, the seller loses nothing. A seller's refusal to do this without a substantial reason is forbidden by the rabbis as *kofin al midat S'dom,* acting in

---

Dislocation has economic, social and environmental aspects. Town centers across America and the world are losing population, business and centrality as suburban ring roads and bypasses sprout box store upon box store. Profits flow out of the community; homogenous products are offered; existing infrastructure is underutilized, while new farmland and forest are paved over; relationships sustained by the intimacy of town centers are strained; the health of democracy is impaired. How do concerns like these fit into the cost-benefit analyses of corporations and even governments? Where do they fit in the decisions we make as Jews, consumers and citizens?   —F.S.D.

The principle that owners of adjacent property should have a first opportunity to buy when an owner wishes to sell makes sense in the context of farming. However, this can be (and has been) used as a justification for sellers in a white neighborhood to avoid selling to potential buyers of a different race. That is clearly an unethical perversion of the principle and its purpose.   —E.Z.

the way that the people of ancient Sodom were reputed to have conducted themselves, acting arbitrarily in ways that hurt others without providing gain to themselves. One should not for the sake of a whim ("I don't like that guy!") refuse an arrangement that would be significantly helpful to someone else. Of course, the seller ought to also consider the effects on third parties of the anticipated use by the potential new owner. The principle involved here is that sellers and buyers are supposed to maximize the overall good within the context of doing business in a way that is good for themselves and one another.

The Buyer's Obligations

When a buyer makes a purchase, that item can only be returned if it is flawed, improperly described, or priced above its fair worth, and then only within a reasonable length of time, unless the seller voluntarily agrees to other terms. If the buyer discovers that the item has far greater worth than the seller understood, the buyer is obliged to return the object or pay the difference, which is not the case in English common law or American practice.

The principle of *tzelem Elohim* allows us to move beyond ego-driven preferences (I like this, I don't like that) to embrace a justice that fosters connection and limits the self-centered ego. —S.P.W.

Shrewd horse-trading was engaged in by the Patriarchs—and by Jews throughout the millennia. I don't think that Jewish ethics negates the search for "bargain sales" or "bargain purchases." —E.Z.

The fair price of an item depends upon the market value and comparability of goods. The advent of trading on the Internet has expanded the size of the market, but comparability is a complex question. A store that provides more selection, a pleasant place to shop and expert service can legitimately charge more than a cut-rate Internet source that provides no such service. If one starts out with the intent to buy on the Internet or from a wholesaler in order to save money but uses the services of a full-service store to select merchandise because the less expensive source does not provide those services, this represents a form of theft. The customer has obtained labor and expertise that are provided to secure a proper purchase under false pretenses because the customer deceived the seller about the customer's intent to consider making a purchase at that store.

Many contemporary stores expect window shopping and encourage browsing because it sometimes leads to purchasing. As long as one does not hide one's intentions, this is legitimate conduct in such stores. It is not acceptable conduct when it means raising the hopes of the proprietor of a small business who has no reason to expect such behavior (Mishna, *Bava Metzia* 4.10). One should take care not to encourage a store's personnel to believe that

I grew up in a retail store in the Bronx that sold carpet, rugs and linoleum. My grandfather, a Russian immigrant, started the business, and my mother, father and two uncles spent their entire working lives in "the business." I would go to the store after school and on Saturdays to be with my mother while she was working. I have a visceral memory of the rhythm of someone looking and buying and someone "just looking." As the rabbi at Friday night services years later, I would have the same feeling of waiting for customers to show up and wondering how many would buy.   —S.P.W.

one will make a purchase in order to get service when that is not a likely outcome of the interaction. Falsely raising the hopes of an owner that a purchase is imminent or using the time of an employee on that basis fraudulently obtains something of value; it is a version of theft by deceit, *g'neyvat da'at*. Telling a salesperson that one wants to look but will not make a decision to buy for quite some time allows the seller to make realistic decisions about how to handle the situation in a way that is in the seller's interest.

Buying a product, using it and then returning it for a full refund when it is no longer needed is a form of theft of service. On the other hand, buying it with the intent to return it if it does not match colors at home or if it is not compatible with home equipment is something to which the store may well agree in advance. Returning merchandise that does not live up to the purpose for which it has been bought is ethical behavior, but it may be subject to store rules or laws that are not reflective of Jewish ethics. Some stores choose to exchange merchandise that has not worn well as a marketing method that generates customer loyalty and future sales.

I am constantly amazed by the depth of the rabbis' ethical insights. One outstanding example is their application of the principle of *g'neyvat da'at* to shopping at a retail location with the explicit purpose of gaining information without having any intention to purchase the item there. —J.N.C.

Transactions Involving Investments

Large purchases, such as land, a business, or a house, often involve negotiating. In the process of bargaining, it is ethical for those on each side of a transaction to attempt to obtain the terms that are most favorable to them. In the process of the negotiation, it is impermissible to lie or to create deceptive perceptions. Bargaining must follow the principle of *hin tzedek,* good faith. No bluffing is allowed in the negotiation because bluffing is always deceptive.

If there is a bidding war, the parameters of that process should be made explicit in order to allow all bidders an equal chance. When a deal is about to be struck, a new potential buyer must not interfere but may do so earlier while negotiations are still underway. If an agreement is reached orally, it is morally binding unless it is explicit that the agreement is not complete until it is written out and signed.

Sellers have an obligation to disclose material defects or conditions of the property that affect its use or value even if the buyer does not elicit the information by asking a question. Such issues might involve zoning, adjacent land uses, the condition of the property and repairs that may be needed, or issues with utilities or sewage, to name but a few. Obviously the seller cannot disclose flaws of which the seller is not aware. The goal is to ensure that the transaction benefits both parties.

I would not think it wrong for a seller to raise the possibility of another buyer appearing as long as the seller was not lying. Similarly, without lying, the buyer may emphasize all that is wrong with the property in question. These do not amount to bluffing. —L.S.

Another common purchase is stock and bonds. Maintaining trading by keeping the market for shares orderly and reasonably stable and ensuring a steady flow of pricing information is a critical part of fairness. Intentionally manipulating the market or trading based on information that is kept secret to prevent the market from reflecting the stock's genuine worth are unethical behaviors. All the relevant information about the companies involved must be reported fully and in a timely manner. This means that people who are not direct parties to a stock trade or bond purchase nonetheless have moral obligations to the buyer and seller to ensure that the transactions are fair. This places a substantial fiduciary responsibility on corporate officers, board members and those charged with stabilizing stock, bond and commodity markets.

Even in transactions that directly involve only the buyer and seller, broader community interests are at stake, such as the maintenance of stable markets, the free flow of goods and efficient distribution. The buyer, seller and other mem-

It is important to distinguish between improper trading in stocks based on "inside information" and the completely ethical practice of trading based on superior research.   —E.Z.

A major question here is the ethics of artificially declaring positive, short-term news when a stock's value is questionable in the longer term. Norms that support such short-term stock gains ultimately create enormous wealth for a small segment of society while weakening society in general.   —N.P.

 here is a long history of Jewish family businesses. What happens when family relations intersect with business relations? Suppose a family business employs and exploits family members to contribute to a family economy or, at the other end of the family business spectrum, suppose extended family members compete for leadership of a company. Should a business be handed down to family members to give them a livelihood, or should it be sold to the highest bidder? There is no single, neat answer to these questions. It depends upon agreements among family members, the wishes of the owners, and the obligations that one would have to employees and co-owners who were not relatives.   —D.D.M.

bers of the community all have an obligation to ensure that the interests of all the stakeholders are reasonably protected.

Leasing and Renting

According to Jewish tradition and most traditional legal approaches, owners have the right to rent or not to rent properties as they choose. They also have the right to rent to whomever they wish, and to select renters using whatever criteria they prefer. Historical Jewish experience, which includes considerable discrimination, indicates the serious problems in such an unconstrained approach. Contemporary Jewish values dictate that owners not discriminate based on sex, gender identity, race, ethnicity, religion, age or sexual orientation.

Owners have the right to propose any reasonable terms in the lease contract for space they are renting. Sometimes a rental market is tight, and they could charge more because one potential renter is particularly desperate to stay in the

Other factors, such as sexual orientation, socio-economic status (unless it pertains to the ability to pay rent), physical appearance, or other presumed differences, should not be used to discriminate. These factors unfortunately can be hidden behind more "reasonable" criteria. —Y.R.

The traditional Jewish texts that inform our values don't always dictate non-discrimination; this *Guide* articulates "contemporary Jewish values" that do. Contemporary Jewish values, somewhat inchoate at this stage, are shaped by our shared understandings of Jewish texts and traditions, by recent communal history, and by secular thought and experience. Attempts to put this all together will be open to argument and to constant reinterpretation. Even so, the open, values-based decision-making model outlined here is invaluable; would that all Jews, and all people, used it. —F.S.D.

The discussion on renting relies on the rabbinic assumption that landlords have the greater power. This may or may not be the case in the contemporary world. For example, a large retail chain tenant usually has greater power than a strip mall owner. —E.Z.

neighborhood for personal reasons, but owners are never allowed to charge more than the fair market value—the amount that other neighborhood renters would pay—for the rental of their property.

People who live for a long period in a rented apartment or house develop friendships and attachments that can make moving difficult and painful. Businesses that rent space often develop good will with customers and suppliers; that good will would not necessarily be of use to them if they were forced to move a long distance away. It is therefore important that owners have the obligation to renew leases at the market rate for the people already renting. Owners must not extort payments above the market value because tenants do not want to move. If an owner requires a renter to leave because the owner wishes to use the property or upgrade it, the renter has the moral right of first refusal when the owner (or even a subsequent owner) puts up the property for rent again.

Owners have an obligation as specified in the lease to maintain their properties in reasonable repair and to provide heat and water as specified. The presumption in a landlord-tenant relationship is that the landlord has greater power, so it is incumbent upon the landlord to ensure that the renter can maintain reasonable use of the property. This does not reduce the right of the landlord to evict, after reasonable warning, a tenant who fails to pay the rent.

If the Earth belongs to God (Psalm 24), to whom we are but strangers and sojourners (Leviticus 25), then all 6.4 billion people today are tenants on God's planet, subject to eviction if we don't keep the place up like we should. Deuteronomy 11, the traditional second paragraph of the *Sh'ma,* offers a dire warning that this eviction could be speedy. We humans have a long way to go if we are to restore balance and live in the light. —F.S.D.

Agents and Brokers

Many transactions involve agents or brokers. These include real estate, stocks, bonds and commodities, as well as other contract negotiations, including employment. Agents have a fiduciary responsibility (additional specific responsibility that flows from the nature of a particular role) to look out for the welfare of their clients even when doing so may not be in the agent's own best interest (*Shulḥan Arukh, Ḥoshen Mishpat* 183–195). If agents are involved, the agreements with the agents should be made clear and explicit regarding services to be rendered, terms, fees and costs. The full situations of both the potential client and the agent should be disclosed so that they both can assess whether their interests coincide sufficiently to make an agreement sensible. Agents have an obligation to disclose the nature of their operations so that potential clients can make an educated judgment as to whether the agent can adequately fulfill the responsibilities intended.

The Special Case of Monopolies

Monopolies raise particular problems in a market economy. They may develop because there is not sufficient business for competing firms, as might be the case with a

According to Jewish tradition, monopolies should be regulated only when they are engaged in unfair practices, such as price gouging. American legal principles presuppose that a deemed monopoly, such as one that might arise out of a merger of two market leaders, is automatically assumed not to be in the commonweal's interest and thus should be barred in advance. The difference stems from the fact that the stance on monopolies in Jewish tradition did not anticipate the scope or behavior of contemporary corporations. —J.N.C.

kosher butcher shop serving a town with barely enough Jews to support it. Monopolies may also develop because there are efficiencies of scale that they achieve, as is the case in providing wiring that carries electricity into every home and business in a city. Monopolies cannot set prices according to a market price because by definition monopolies have no market competition. They are therefore in a position where they can charge exploitatively for their goods or fail to provide the quality of service that the buyer or consumer should reasonably be able to expect. Monopolies are entitled to make a fair profit but not an excessive one, and should provide goods of reasonable quality. Where monopolies fail to meet these moral obligations, it is not surprising that they become subject to government regulation, which is often expensive, unwieldy and subject to politics, but far better than the consequences that flow from failing to regulate an unscrupulous monopoly.

When the rabbinic courts in medieval times had the power to do so, they recognized that someone running a business just large enough to survive (like a local kosher butcher shop) deserved the protection of the court against someone new moving in (*ḥerem hayishuv*), undercutting the price and driving the original butcher out of business. The courts acted on the resident butcher's behalf because they saw the *kavod* and livelihood of the butcher and the fabric of the community as more important than a slight

---

The kosher butcher has a distinct responsibility as a business owner to preserve a communal halakhic standard. If a desire to offer better deals undermines fastidious attention to the laws of *kashrut,* it will be impossible for the business to maintain a good reputation or even stay in business.   —N.H.M.

and perhaps short-term savings to the customers. But where the local butcher had been warned about the quality or cleanliness of the business and the butcher had not heeded the warning, the rabbis permitted a new butcher to move in. While these arrangements only pertained to those businesses where Jewish courts could exercise control, they establish the obligations of monopolies as well as the value placed on the continuity of relationships and the dignity of individual workers over maximizing economic efficiency. The intrinsic, non-economic goods must be balanced against the extrinsic economic ones.

Borrowing and Investing

In biblical times, borrowing among Israelites was done on an interest-free basis (Exodus 22:24), and lending at interest was forbidden because in that simple agricultural situation, it involved exploitation of the poor, who borrowed in order to eat. Furthermore, all debts were cancelled in the seventh year. By rabbinic times, lending money had become part of commerce, and the Jews' inability to lend money to each other hampered their capacity to conduct business. Hillel's innovative *prosbol* (a ruling he issued a generation before the destruction of the Second Temple) limited the restrictions on lending by circumventing the seventh-year rule through involvement of the courts (see B. Talmud *Gittin* 36a-b), albeit with some halakhic constraints. The complexities that arise from these halakhic constraints have resulted in a voluminous halakhic literature that narrows them as much as possible. In their present form, these inherited restraints are not about ethics.

From a Jewish ethical perspective, lending and borrowing money for a variety of purposes at a reasonable rate of interest is a legitimate and indeed critical function in contemporary economies. Without it, home buying, launching or expanding a business and bridging unforeseen difficulties would be impossible for most people.

What constitutes a fair rate of interest? To a considerable extent, that is established by market conditions. However, it is reasonable that a lender who undertakes a greater risk lender should receive a greater return. On the other hand, usurious rates of interest are unethical. A loan given in anticipation that the borrower will not be able to keep up the payments is usurious by nature. The line between a legitimate high-risk loan and a predatory, usurious one varies in time and place; often that line is determined by

In fact, borrowing money responsibly is one of the primary means for middle class Americans and others to build wealth and establish financial stability through home-ownership. —A.A.

A contemporary example of exploitation, which also violates the caveat against putting a stumbling block before the blind, is the proliferation of unsolicited credit card offers that are often sent to individuals like college seniors and people who have bad credit histories. This often results in individuals starting credit lines without a clear understanding of the responsibility this entails. —N.H.M.

It is interesting to note that adherence to the principle that "a loan given in anticipation that the borrower will not be able to keep up the payments is usurious by nature" would have put significant breaks on the uncontrolled growth in the American sub-prime mortgage market and its subsequent implosion in 2007. —J.N.C.

There are other, more common indicators of impropriety on the part of a lender, such as efforts to promote loans to vulnerable populations and deceitful behavior to convince lenders that their proposed loan payments are viable. —S.P.W.

law. One clear indicator of unethical, predatory behavior is the threat or use of force to collect overdue debts.

The lender has an obligation to make explicit the terms of the loan, including arrangements for handling collateral, interest rates, schedule of payments and penalties for nonpayment. A lender should not seize collateral that will leave the borrower destitute (Exodus 22:25–26). Borrowers have an obligation not to borrow money if they are not reasonably certain that they will be able to repay the loan.

Buying bonds is a form of lending money. The risks and profits are parallel, with riskier bonds paying higher rates of interest. The same ethical standards apply whether a loan is made privately, through a bank or another commercial lender, or through a bond regulated by industry or government standards.

In sharp contrast to Roman law and various medieval European legal systems, the debtor never risked physical punishment for non-payment according to biblical and rabbinic law.   —L.K.

The importance given to *kavod* in the tradition is reflected in Deuteronomy 24:10, which bars the creditor from entering the debtor's house to collect a pledge.   —L.K.

The Center for Responsible Lending has established seven signs that a loan is predatory in present-day U.S. practice: excessive fees, abusive prepayment penalties, kickbacks to brokers, loan flipping, unnecessary products, mandatory arbitration, and steering and targeting. These practices have caused many households to lose their homes and have stripped communities and households of wealth. Although a few states have laws against these practices, there is no federal law or regulation at this time.   —A.A.

Bankruptcy laws were instituted to allow a debtor who was unable to pay to have a fresh start. In the words of Deuteronomy 15:1, "At the end of every seven years shall you make a release."   —L.K.

One who invests in a business directly as a silent partner or as an owner of shares of stock is subject to the profits and losses of the business, which are allocated according to the amount of the investment. These investments are frequently needed for the benefit of owners, employees and society more broadly. With such investments, the possibility of both risk and profit are greater than with bonds. The need for such investment has increased over time. Capital is needed in unprecedented amounts by businesses shaped by international corporations with vast technological sophistication. The existence of huge, complex corporations over which the ordinary investor can exercise little control beyond buying or selling stock has led to a shift in moral responsibility regarding these investments to corporate boards. These boards have the complex task of balancing the rights and obligations of all the corporation's stakeholders. The members of such boards have a primary obligation to these stakeholders. Board members must avoid the kind of informal collusion with corporate management that can easily result from the intimate associations that inevitably accompany the roles of senior executives and board members in such corporations.

We get into trouble when "stakeholder" becomes shorthand for "shareholder." A relatively small number of people directly profit from a company's financial success. A company's board of directors has responsibility for a much broader impact. I believe that stakeholders include every person, both near and far, as well as people living in the future and the rest of the animal, vegetable, and mineral world. Corporations are not immoral per se, but by that standard they are largely amoral—an approach that is incompatible with the Jewish one, which places morality at the center.   —F.S.D.

Some ethicists have argued that insider-trading practices do not really have deleterious consequences judging by their effect on the preservation of well-functioning markets. Some make similar arguments about backdating options: "Who suffers?" Jewish adherence to underlying ethical principles, on the other hand, clearly distinguishes such behavior as immoral.   —J.N.C.

Many additional forms of investment have developed in response to complex economic needs. These include commodities markets, currency and other forms of arbitrage, futures, puts and calls, and selling short, to name but a few. When such tools have a legitimate economic function, investing is an ethical economic activity provided that the investor does not engage in such unethical activities as intentional market manipulation or improper use of information (as in insider trading).

One of the obligations of investors is to ensure that their investments are used to further ethical behavior. If the investment supports a business that mistreats workers, squanders natural resources, encourages unhealthy behavior, or otherwise behaves in an antisocial manner, then the investor must either use that investment as leverage to eliminate that unethical behavior, or the investor must divest. Otherwise the investor is abetting unethical behavior by providing the capital that helps it to occur. Holders of investments such as mutual funds will have a much more difficult time in deciding when this applies to them

Socially responsible investing is a burgeoning field. At a minimum it seeks to screen out the worst companies on issues like product safety and health (e.g. smoking and gun manufacturing), environmental practices and treatment of workers. More sophisticated socially responsible investing approaches actively encourage the best up-and-comers, enabling more windmills to be built and more environmental remediation to occur. Really, who wants socially irresponsible investments?   —F.S.D.

How should the investor arrive at a balanced answer about the contours of the obligation to divest? For example, when is an investor obligated to divest his investment in a company that sells tobacco products, is cited for environmental violations, cuts forest lands for private gain or invests in countries that are governed by dictatorships? These are complex questions requiring careful investigation and analysis, and ethical people will not all reach the same conclusions. However, ignoring these questions is certainly unethical.   —L.S.

because mutual funds often hold shares in dozens of corporations. While mutual fund shareholders will therefore not necessarily be able to identify every investment that involves unethical behavior, they should certainly act when they become aware of such a holding. A first step would be to encourage the mutual fund to use its leverage—which is usually far greater than that of an ordinary investor because of the size of mutual fund holdings—to move the offending corporation toward a change in policy. In many cases, the holdings by mutual funds and pension funds are vast. These funds have the same obligations as private citizens in regard to ensuring ethical behavior by corporations.

Given the nature of investing, government regulation is needed to protect all concerned. Those involved with investing have an obligation to work to ensure that regulatory systems are as fair and efficient as possible.

Although "ethical investing" has existed as a concept for over 30 years, it is still a fringe practice among mutual fund traders. Most wealth managers neither concern themselves with social agendas nor recognize that investors may want their money to support environmental efforts or at least not to fund war efforts.   —N.P.

Many current investment options adhere to standards of socially responsible investing and have track records of performance across a wide range of market environments. However, the definition of "socially responsible" is broad, and each investment adviser uses individualized screens to determine whether an investment meets a particular set of requirements. Tools are available on the Web to evaluate the range of investment options and their screens to ensure that your investments reflect your wishes. One argument against socially responsible investing is that it potentially limits investment returns by limiting the range of investment choices. However, recent academic studies have shown that socially responsible investment options have produced competitive returns compared to those options that do not use a socially responsible screen. There are now few barriers to investing on an ethical or socially responsible basis.   —M.N.

There are many socially responsible mutual funds available that will not invest in industries or companies that they consider unethical.   —A.A.

Advice and Consulting

Those who offer advice take the risk that their advice will be followed and that they will bear some culpability for the results. Thus people who are asked advice have an obligation to be explicit about what they know and how they are applying that knowledge to a particular case. If they do not have extensive experience, they should say so, thereby providing the advice seeker with sufficient background to determine the value of the advice. One who gives advice without having sufficient knowledge and experience is guilty of putting a stumbling block before the blind.

Consultants earn their living through their knowledge, capacity for analysis and interpersonal skills. Just as with material merchandise, the seller—in this case the consultant—has an obligation to disclose the soundness of the merchandise and its suitability for a particular use. Consultants have a fiduciary responsibility to look out for the best interests of their clients, and that includes protecting clients from the pitfalls of receiving advice that is outside the consultants' areas of competence. If consultants

While the consultant has to be scrupulously truthful, it would be mutually disadvantageous to present things in a way that would result in every potential client walking away. Nevertheless, it is important for the consultant to state clearly the extent to which the results of following the advice are iffy or subject to uncontrolled variables. The consultant should be very clear if the results of following the advice are not certain.   —L.S.

Many professions potentially involve conflicts of interest. When one is earning a profit by providing expert advice, standards of ethical behavior must be clearly articulated and followed at all times. In any situation with a conflict of interest, it is essential to fully disclose all potential conflicts upfront, so that everyone is fully informed as to the nature of the conflict. Ethical professionals always put their clients' interests ahead of their own.   —M.N.

promise more than they can deliver or provide advice that is insufficiently expert, they are morally responsible both for receiving money under false pretenses and for the actions that others take based on their words and deeds.

Thus Jewish thought holds advisers—and consultants even more so because of their fiduciary responsibility to their clients—responsible for the consequences of the advice they give. When this stance is put in the context of the Jewish commitments to truth-telling and to doing business in a way that benefits both sides of a transaction, this approach reflects the internal consistency of Jewish business ethics.

Bankruptcy

Individuals, families and companies become bankrupt when their liabilities exceed their assets, and foreseeable income is not large enough to close the gap. This situation results in creditors not receiving all to which they are entitled. When this tragic situation occurs, creditors have a claim on a percentage of the assets proportional to the amount they are owed regardless of when the debt was incurred.

An expert's advice in the context of economic and organizational transactions is completely different from the advice that a rabbi might offer on a moral question. In traditional settings, when someone asks a rabbi for a ruling on a matter of Jewish law, the asking presumes consequent compliance on the part of the person submitting the inquiry. In such settings, rabbis would indeed be responsible for the consequences of the opinions they render, and as a matter of Jewish law, it would not just be advice. But in Jewish spiritual settings where Jewish law is not presumed as the ultimate arbiter, the kind of spiritual or theological advice a rabbi might offer is in the context of teaching or counseling. The decision whether to follow, or act upon, the rabbi's advice or suggestion rests with the other person. It is incumbent on rabbis (just as it is on psychotherapists) to remind people that ultimately they are responsible for their choices and actions.   —R.H.

Once persons or organizations have the first glimmer that bankruptcy is a real possibility for them, they are morally obligated not to make gifts or significant dowries, or to spend lavishly on entertainment or travel because the assets being spent may not be their own. Such spending is a form of theft. Anyone who has recently received a gift from a person or organization that subsequently goes bankrupt must return the gift because the debtor was giving away property that rightly belonged to the creditors.

According to Jewish ethics, a bankrupt person whose assets have been divided by creditors is not thereby absolved of repaying the remainder of the debt. If the debtor's fortunes should improve, that person is morally bound to gradually pay off the remainder of the debts as conditions allow. The debtor must decide to make personal sacrifices to accomplish this because legal protec-

I have much greater sympathy with the historical Jewish approach regarding bankruptcy than I do with the approach in Anglo-Saxon common law. The Jewish approach says that if debtors' fortunes improve, they are morally bound to repay the debts they incurred before their bankruptcy. Anglo-Saxon common law permits bankrupt persons to expunge significant portions of their debts. Under the provisions of the recently enacted U.S. bankruptcy code, those who are declare bankruptcy have far less wiggle room to free themselves from all obligations than had previously been the case.   —J.N.C.

How much personal sacrifice should there be to pay off debts? Should an individual use family money set aside for children's education or for a *sima* like a wedding? Sell a family home or liquidate retirement savings? Preserving the *kavod* of the individual and the family requires both living decently and repaying debts.   —D.D.M.

The whole point of Chapter X and Chapter XI reorganizations in American law—as well as of the seventh-year and 50th-year Jewish laws—is precisely to give the debtor a totally fresh start without prior encumbrances. Certainly many debtors abuse this privilege, some even declaring bankruptcy repeatedly. But a genuinely bankrupt person should not be forever indebted to his prior creditors.   —E.Z.

tions in most places bar creditors from pursuing the debtor for payment once the liquidation of assets that accompanies bankruptcy has occurred. One who does not repay such debts is regarded as a thief. (Much of the material about bankruptcy comes from the medieval period or later. See, for example, *Va'ad Arba Aratzot, Pikras* 126, regulations from the East European Jewish community.)

Not-For-Profit Organizations

Not-for-profit organizations have several characteristics that make them different from for-profit businesses. Not-for-profits are supported by *tzedaka,* foundation grants and other public monies, and their goal is solely to serve the public good rather than to make a profit. A not-for-profit must therefore balance the fulfillment of its mission with a variety of ethical considerations regarding its ongo-

Bankruptcy claims by American airlines have been used to justify the reduction and even the elimination of pension payments and health insurance for retired workers who worked with the understanding that the companies would pay these benefits during their retirement years. Improper use of bankruptcy law to avoid such moral obligations is, sadly, gaining momentum.   —N.P.

The not-for-profit world applies business models, benchmarks and approaches drawn from the private sector. Not for-profit organizations like synagogues can certainly learn a thing or two about efficiency. The learning has great potential in both directions because the day-to-day concerns and realities of a CEO or a business lawyer diverge greatly from those of an educator or a clergyperson. The dialogue can bring much to both parties, as long as all who participate are willing to explore their assumptions as part of the process.   —F.S.D.

ing operations. These include all the considerations facing businesses discussed above, plus the obligation to use public funds with maximal efficiency. These three concerns—mission, efficiency and the concerns of business ethics—are in direct tension with each other.

One valuable tool that not-for-profits can use effectively when deciding how to operate is a list of organizational values. These are not determinative of the organization's mission, but they can guide decisions and shape the ongoing practices of the organization. Such a list is also helpful in orienting new volunteers and staff members to the culture and procedures of the organization. (For a list of values with definitions, see the "Attitude, Beliefs, and Values" section of this *Guide,* originally published in the same volume as *"Kashrut."*)

The extent to which not-for-profit organizations and business enterprises share the same obligations is striking. The avoidance of conflicts of interest, the safeguarding of worker *kavod* and the protection and wise use of assets are all obligations (and goals) of both not-for-profit and for-profit enterprises. Yet the limelight is more sharply on the not-for-profit organizations, perhaps because they are supposed "to do good" and their failings are violations of the public trust and a form of hypocrisy.   —L.S.

Synagogues are organized to serve the spiritual, educational and communal needs of Jews. The people who undertake the creation of a congregation do not usually do so for the sake of establishing a business. Nonetheless, some part of running the congregation involves doing business: hiring and firing employees; insuring compliance with building, safety and access codes; and managing income and expenses in a responsible manner, to name a few. But because synagogues are normally incorporated as not-for-profit organizations, the "bottom line" ought to be consistent with the noble and elevated purposes for which the congregation was created. Spiritually speaking, synagogues are "for prophet" organizations.   —R.H.

Synagogues that communally shape their norms and expectations based on shared values and vision thereby create an identity for the congregation. When new members join, they know just what kind of congregation they are joining, and by voluntarily affiliating they are implicitly agreeing to shape their Jewish behavior within the norms of the community.   —R.H.

Because not-for-profit organizations benefit from public funds and *tzedaka* support, they have an obligation to avoid not only impropriety but also the appearance of impropriety, *marit ayin*. All employees and volunteers have fiduciary responsibilities as a result of their roles in the organization to ensure that the resources of the organization are properly used and that the organization behaves in a morally exemplary way. One application of this concern is the obligation to ensure that board members and appropriate staff have records free of moral violations and legal convictions relevant to their positions. An organizational policy should require such leaders to step aside from the time they are accused of a crime that would disqualify them for their positions until they are found innocent. Having a policy in advance avoids having to develop an approach when there is a particular person under discussion.

Conflicts of interest are a common occurrence in not-for-profit governance because the involvements of not-for-profit leaders are often complex and multifaceted. Anyone with a conflict of interest has an obligation, upon

---

Are synagogue dues a form of *tzedaka?* Rabbi Mordechai Liebling says that dues are not a form of *tzedaka* "because dues support an institution that we need to fulfill our duties as Jews." See the discussion in the *Tzedaka* section of *A Guide to Jewish Practice.* —R.H.

Board members also have a fiduciary responsibility not only to avoid conflicts of interest, but to also follow the higher standard of avoiding even the appearance of a conflict of interest. A conflict of interest occurs when the interest of the individual and the interest of the organization are not the same. Many individuals serve on the boards of synagogues and other not-for-profit organizations. In their roles as board members, they should not seek to do any business with the organization or provide any services for a fee. And they should be careful to make decisions that place the interests of the organization ahead of their personal wishes and desires. —M.N.

first recognizing the conflict, to disclose that conflict to everyone involved in related decision making. This is true even for a minor conflict of interest. If the conflict might affect an outcome or appear to do so, those involved must absent themselves from the group not only during the voting but from all of the relevant discussion as well. This will help to avoid impropriety and, almost as important, help to avoid any public doubt about the integrity of the organization.

Not-for-profit organizations have the same obligation as other individuals and organizations to safeguard worker dignity and provide suitable compensation. One key part of proper employee treatment is fair and effective evaluation of employee performance. Organizations should ensure that evaluations are not arbitrary, that they are appropriate to the nature of the work, and that they are done with generosity of spirit and good will while also honestly assessing substantial issues. Good evaluation is critical to the sound functioning and proper stewardship of not-for-profit organizations.

Since congregations are not-for-profit organizations, clear and consistent performance reviews of their staff members, rabbis and cantors ought to be the norm.   —N.P.

Professional evaluation is an ongoing tool for a healthy rabbi-congregation relationship. Poorly planned and executed performance evaluations often do more to subvert and destroy good rabbi-congregation relationships than any other factor. They too often become popularity contests, or proxy votes on rehiring, or simply an opportunity by way of an inappropriate and unhelpful congregational survey for people to take shots at the rabbi. For guidance, see "The Rabbi Congregation Relationship: A Vision for the 21st Century."   —R.H.

Evaluation is a critical element of employee respect. Unfortunately this torah is neither taught nor practiced widely enough in Jewish communities.   —S.P.W.

It is often the case that new not-for-profits as well as highly ideological ones have workers who are extremely devoted. This can lead to worker exploitation (e.g. inhumanely long hours, pay lower than a living wage, and/or lack of appropriate benefits). The boards of not-for-profits have an obligation to avoid engaging in this exploitation even if the workers are committed enough that they do not protest. Fulfilling the mission should not come at the cost of exploiting workers.

On the other hand, large, long-established not-for-profits sometimes develop complex bureaucracies that are not very efficient. They often act in preservation of the bureaucracy instead of in the interest of the efficient and effective fulfillment of their missions. This is an abuse of the public trust that the board and staff are responsible for preventing. The effective use of funds to retain excellent personnel and suitable equipment is necessary for the organization to do its best work, but preserving the public trust requires proper monitoring of expense accounts and avoidance of unnecessary expenditures when expending *tzedaka* funds.

The lines that separate for-profit organizations from not-for-profit organizations have become thinner than ever before. There are, for example, for-profit and not-for-profit hospitals, gift shops and publishers. Not-for-profits compete with each other and with for-profit organizations for market share and income. When such competition is unavoidable, it must take place with scrupulous attention to ethical standards regarding honesty, disclosure and the avoidance of gossip.

Board members of not-for-profit organizations, including congregations, should do what they can to ensure that employees do not overwork to the employees' detriment. —N.P.

Not-for-profit organizations, like all organizations, exist amid a turbulent and ever-changing environment. External forces often negatively impact the organization's capacity to fulfill its mission or to function effectively. When such circumstances occur, the organization and its leaders have an obligation to face them as soon as possible. The organization may be able to adjust its course and renew the effective, efficient fulfillment of a meaningful purpose. When that is not the case, the organization ought to consider relocation, merger or dissolution, undertaking the exploration of its options in a timely way that avoids unintentionally squandering the organization's assets. Such assets ultimately belong to the whole community and are placed in the hands of the not-for-profit to serve the common good.

Not-for-profits are often major investors because they control endowment funds. Investment policies and procedures require ongoing monitoring to ensure prudent investing that reflects the organization's short-term and long-term interests. The investments in the organization's portfolio ought to be examined to ensure that they do not conflict with the mission or values of the organization. Every part of the not-for-profit should be able to withstand close scrutiny regarding mission, values, effectiveness and efficiency. Investments by not-for-profits should reflect a focus on serving the common good.

Foundations form one important class of not-for-profit organizations. A foundation is often controlled by the family that creates it, or sometimes by members of an extended family and their friends. Regardless of where the money in the foundation came from, the foundation is a public trust, and its resources must be used to serve the community rather than the sometimes self-serving wishes of those who created it. Of course thoughtful people will differ about the best uses of the funds. Developing criteria for allocating grants and following them carefully, along with assuring that grantees will be effective at fulfilling their grants, helps to minimize the way that personal preferences and relationships can negatively affect judgments in the granting process. Like all other not-for-profit organizations, foundations have an obligation to function both efficiently and effectively. In the course of doing their work, they have an obligation to protect the dignity of all the different individuals and organizations with which they interact, and to create processes that avoid inadvertently wasting the resources—money, time, energy and ideas—of the grantees and grant applicants with whom they deal.

Membership organizations should ensure that members are treated respectfully and that anyone who embarrasses members is dealt with effectively to prevent recurrences.

Synagogues struggle with a variety of models for fair dues assessments. For a helpful discussion, see the article by Rabbi Shawn Zevit, "Synagogue Dues with Less Blues." While almost every congregation makes allowances for dues adjustment based on need, we have yet to devise a model that avoids some degree of embarrassment for the congregant who makes such a request. —R.H.

Like other membership organizations that offer dues adjustments in good faith, synagogues face instances where congregants who are well-positioned to pay full dues define those dues as a choice rather than as an obligation and who self-assess based on how much they value their involvement. Dues, however, support the synagogue based on its usefulness to the community as a whole. When a congregant or congregant family asks for a reduction in dues, it might be helpful to imagine they are asking each congregant, not the synagogue treasurer. If in good conscience they can imagine looking other congregants in the eye, knowing that some of them in more challenging circumstances are in fact paying full dues, and still feel it is appropriate in their situation to ask for a reduction in dues, then they should ask. —R.H.

Such organizations also should ensure that dues and fees are fairly assessed and that those who deserve reductions in dues and fees because of need are treated in a way that preserves their dignity.

Jewish organizations have an obligation to govern themselves within the parameters established by Jewish ethics. The leaders of such organizations have generally not learned Jewish business ethics, and they do not necessarily practice them in their everyday lives. For Jewish organizations to follow Jewish ethics, their boards and senior employees must develop familiarity with those parameters. This does not occur by itself, so these organizations have an obligation to provide their leaders with a sufficient education in these matters so that they can properly execute their fiduciary responsibilities. The obligation to undertake moral education and other forms of staff and leadership development falls particularly on the board chair and the executive director, who must ensure that such leadership training is conducted on a regular basis.

In my experience (e.g., as president of my congregation), the problem has not been about embarrassing people who need dues reductions. It is that people who can afford to pay often don't, or they pay late, or they claim they can't afford it and take advantage of the Jewish ethic that causes us to refrain from making them prove they can't afford it.   —E.Z.

One excellent way to fairly assess dues and fees is to make them "fair-share"—with progressive, graduated, percentage-of-income assessments on each member of a community. Many synagogues and other agencies have already made the transition to that system, while others, with real trepidation around budgeting and solvency during the early years of the new model, contemplate it.   —F.S.D.

Synagogues and other Jewish organizations can establish a legal claim to the payment of a pledge. Should they utilize legally binding pledges? If a donor recants, should legal steps be taken?   —R.H.

I love the idea of making a course on Jewish leadership ethics a requirement for service on all kinds of Jewish boards. It would be like requiring a driver's license.   —S.P.W.

Gifts, Wills, Bequests, and Trusts

Individuals who own property and have paid any required taxes on it have the right to dispose of it as they choose as long as the method of disposal is not inimical to the community interest, as it would be, for example, if it resulted in a zoning violation. Assuming that a person is not in danger of bankruptcy and is fulfilling the obligation to give *tzedaka,* that person can legitimately choose to make gifts of any kind. Similarly individuals can divide their estates or leave them entirely to anyone they choose. Leaving clear instructions in this regard is a moral imperative because failing to do so can cause enmity and hurt feelings, and can result in the squandering of assets (a violation of *bal tash'ḥit,* the rabbinic principle against waste often cited by Jewish environmentalists) that would not have taken place if a clear, legal will had been executed.

When making decisions about who should inherit, it is helpful to keep certain questions in mind. Who needs the money? Who will use the assets wisely? Who deserves an inheritance, and how much do they deserve? How can the assets be divided in a way that minimizes future rancor? How can the relationship between the person creating the will and the inheritor best be memorialized? How does fairness fit in? When should assets be transferred in order to ensure that they are not wasted and that they do not corrupt the recipient? Who can best serve as executor of the will? Family dynamics and individual circumstances differ. Some issues about distributing wealth are treated in the *Tzedaka* section of *A Guide to Jewish Practice.*

Those who fail to leave clear instructions regarding their estates risk creating a situation that threatens the *sh'lom bayit* of their families.   —N.H.M.

When a will specifies that the assets are to be divided on a percentage basis among the inheritors, there are often multiple ways for them to be distributed. While it is of paramount importance for all involved to receive their fair shares, deciding who will get what must be done on an individual basis. Jewish tradition warns that if a particular part of the estate has more value to one inheritor than to another, people should receive the parts uniquely important to them as long as everyone else gets a fair share. Abandoning this principle because of whims or interpersonal conflicts is described by the rabbis as *kofin al midat S'dom,* acting in the inappropriate manner attributed by the rabbis to the ancient dwellers of Sodom (see B. Talmud, *Bava Batra* 12b).

When assets are left in trust to a minor, a trustee stewards the assets until the minor reaches the age required in the will or trust agreement, or reaches the age of majority as defined by local law. The trustee has all the responsibilities of an agent to safeguard the assets, oversee their investment and use them appropriately on the child's behalf. When a significant amount of money is involved, this can create a powerful temptation for the trustee to seek personal advantage. Seeking such advantage is a profound moral violation of the trustee's fiduciary responsibility. Choosing trustees with care is the best protection against such improprieties.

Pursuing Justice

One of the most oft-quoted verses in the Bible proclaims, "*Tzedek, tzedek tirdof*—You shall surely pursue justice" (Deuteronomy 16:20). The rabbis taught that this is an example of *imitatio Dei,* of imitating God's behavior, because God is just. The rabbis portray God as balancing *din,* strict, retributive justice, with *raḥamim,* mercy. The Bible repeatedly calls upon us to care for widows, orphans, the downtrodden and the foreigner as required by justice, which is repeatedly tied to insights based on empathy— "You were slaves in Egypt." The word "*tzedek,*" which can also be translated as "righteousness," can refer to processes, to conduct and to outcomes that are just.

While pursuing justice is one of the main preoccupations of Jewish tradition, Jews have never viewed justice as solely a Jewish concern. The Noahide laws (derived by the

Rashi, an 11ᵗʰ century French biblical and talmudic commentator, famously commented on the repetition of "*tzedek*" in *tzedek, tzedek tirdof.* He suggested that it is said once for means, and once for ends, both of which must be just. Rabbi David Saperstein (director of the Religious Action Center of Reform Judaism) has warned of the "*tzedek* trap," in which we find ourselves leaning too heavily on this verse and testifying that "since our tradition bids us to pursue justice, we favor House Resolution 3274. . . ." *Tzedek tzedek tirdof* should in fact be a meta-value for us, but only with the texture and richness of the millennia of our people added to it.   —F.S.D.

Pirkey Avot (5.13) famously notes that what most people see as a regular everyday approach to the world—"what's mine is mine and what's yours is yours"—at least one Jewish tradition calls the character of Sodom. According to this minority opinion that has been maintained for two millennia, those who simply do the obvious and divide up the material world on the basis of possession may actually be contributing to—or even deserving of—destruction.   —F.S.D.

early rabbis from the story of Noah in Genesis and traditionally regarded as binding on all humanity) include the creation of courts to guarantee the proper administration of justice. Human society cannot be sustained without a method for pursuing justice.

Acting justly is not a simple matter for an individual, but it is more difficult for an organization, even more difficult for a community, and still more difficult for a nation. One reason for this is that the idea of justice rests upon a complex series of assumptions and beliefs. Three principles deserve direct mention: First, we have personal rights regarding our bodies and minds. Second, we have property rights that are an extension of our personal rights. Third, those who violate our rights ought to make restitution and in some cases deserve to be punished. From these three principles can be derived others, such as the right of individuals to act collectively on their own behalf and to create vehicles for the administration of justice. Indeed, Jewish tradition sees the community as having an obligation to ensure justice in human affairs, including economic justice.

Examining all possible applications of these assumptions and beliefs about justice is a task so vast that it could never be completed. The sections that follow sketch some of the fundamental applications of justice, and they should be understood in light of what has been said about justice above. These sections give important examples of how the Jewish approach to justice is applied, but they flesh out the Jewish approach to justice without dealing with every possible circumstance. Nevertheless, they provide sufficient guidance to suggest just approaches to a multitude of issues.

Taxation

The community has the right to tax individuals to ensure health and safety through the provision of community health services, drainage ditches, roads, bridges and so on. The community must also provide the means for commerce and interpersonal connections by building roads and overseeing markets, for example. The community also has an obligation to ensure that people receive adequate food, clothing, medical care and shelter in ways that do not undermine their *kavod*. The community must also protect its members from criminals and invaders. Furthermore, the community has an obligation to ensure the education of children.

When the Jewish community was self-governing during medieval times and earlier, it met most of these obligations on its own. Now that Jews are citizens of secular nations, many of these obligations are fulfilled by the secular government. This necessitates the imposition of taxes, including sales taxes, income taxes, property taxes, inheritance taxes, head taxes (a flat amount assessed on every adult) and so on. As long as these taxes do not overburden the poor, they are permitted, and to the extent that they are needed for the community to meet its basic obliga-

During the earliest stages of Israel's communal life, our ancestors maintained a vision of voluntary gifts to build and sustain the sanctuary. It was only later that a taxation system was imposed.   —T.K.

Rabbi Mordecai Kaplan, the founder of Reconstructionist Judaism, had a vision of an organic Jewish community in which members in effect paid a "tax" in return for which they would have access to all the functions and services of the community.   —R.H.

tions, they are required. Cheating on taxes is a form of theft.

Given the value that Jews place upon meeting the community's obligations to individuals, it is natural that Jews should support universal healthcare insurance (see the discussion in the *Bioethics* section of *A Guide to Jewish Practice*) and related health measures. Most Jews also support ample funding for public schools, solid funding of government pensions (in the United States, Social Security), adequate places to shelter the homeless, soup kitchens, food supplements for needy individuals and families, job creation, job training and other measures that strengthen the general social welfare. While these measures inevitably result in increased government spending and therefore increased taxation, Jewish ethics perceives the provision of such measures as necessary for meeting society's obligations. The money needed to fulfill these mitzvot ought to be collected as taxes. The state should then use that money to meet those community needs.

Doing the wrong thing is never ethical, even if there is a low probability of being caught or if the penalty is modest. Unethical behavior includes evading responsibility for the upkeep of the community by cheating on your taxes, either by under-reporting income (a felony) or claiming excessive and illegitimate deductions. Many people argue that because they are not literally breaking the law or regulation, they are behaving ethically. However, violating the spirit of the law or regulation can be unethical, and doing the right thing often requires more of us than simply obeying the law.   —M.N.

Many inequities arise from the present formula for funding American public schools. Programs such as Teach For America attempt to eliminate these educational inequalities.   —D.E.

Taxation of corporations has decreased, reflecting a conservative view that corporations, more than individuals, have a right to determine their own spending rather than paying taxes. The implications of that thinking fly in the face of Jewish ethics.   —N.P.

Most nations do not yet fulfill all these moral obligations. In such cases, it is incumbent upon the Jewish community to meet the needs of its own members in the interim, but it is extremely difficult to meet these needs without a system of taxation. Jews therefore ought to join with others in efforts to ensure that the governments where they live—including Israel—meet these obligations for all citizens.

Zoning and Property Rights

It is in the overall interest of a community to regulate the use of land even though this reduces the rights of property owners. It is appropriate, for example, to have regulations that prohibit a car-repair shop from opening in the middle of a residential neighborhood because of the noise and smells, or that prohibit a retail shop from operating in a residential neighborhood because of the traffic the shop might generate. Such zoning must not restrict quiet activities that do not cause problems for nearby residents

---

In the building of the *Mishkan,* the Jewish community raised money in two ways: from a half-shekel head tax and from gifts given when the donor was moved to do so. Today, our taxes support a wide range of communal activities, and leaders must often make hard choices about how to allocate scarce resources to meet competing needs. Ethical individuals have an additional responsibility to provide financial support through *tzedaka* to those areas that they believe are most in need. This *tzedaka* provides funds over and above the communal taxes assessed.   —M.N.

Many congregations have become involved in zoning fights when seeking to build or buy a building in proximity to a residential neighborhood. Sometimes the issue is traffic, but often it involves anti-Semitism. Such protracted disputes can significantly disrupt the good will on which communities rely, and residual bad feelings can take a long time to heal.   —R.H.

because that would be an infringement of the owner's rights without a larger gain for the community. This idea could be applied to permit homeowners to add mother-in-law apartments to their homes while prohibiting the renting of homes to a group of unrelated people. That rule would block college-student tenants from having noisy parties in residential areas.

Some rights are understood as developing implicitly. Jewish tradition treats a use that has existed over time as developing into a right. For example, if a family put a hot-tub on their secluded back porch, their neighbor would not be allowed to later put in a new window that would afford the neighbor a view that would interfere with the hot-tub owner's privacy rights. If a farmer has a field that can be accessed only by using an existing private road on an adjacent farm, the adjacent owner cannot deny the farmer the right to use the road unless the owner would incur is a real cost because of the farmer's use. If the farmer offers to pay the real cost, the owner must accept payment and allow use of the road.

Communities also have the right to block land uses and economic production that are not in the interest of the

---

The hot-tub example is a modern-day illustration of Mishna *Bava Batra* 3:7: "No one shall open up windows facing a jointly owned courtyard. . . . No one may place an entrance in a courtyard opposite the entrance (of another) nor a window opposite (another's) window." —L.K.

"And Balaam looked up and saw Israel dwelling tribe by tribe" (Numbers 24:2). The sages explain that Balaam saw that the entrances to the Israelites' tents did not face each other, and this caused him to say "These people are worthy that the Divine Presence should abide with them" (Talmud *Bava Batra* 60a). —L.K.

community. A government that buys land through foreclosure—a procedure known as eminent domain—in order to create a national park is demonstrating one legitimate use of this principle. It can also be applied to banning practices that produce excessive pollution, blocking the dumping of toxic chemicals, or requiring the use of recycling. This is so because the community often bears indirect costs for economic production. The community has the right to demand that producers pay for these costs. When the community does so, this encourages better economic decisions because those decisions are based on the full, actual cost of economic production. When decisions are based only on the direct, short-term cost to the producer, this can result in a calculus that Jewish tradition calls *me'ula b'damim*, improper, exploitative use. Similar logic should also be applied to such decisions as the means of energy production and the cutting of first-growth forests.

Communities can abuse the right to block land use by promulgating laws that would keep out groups they deem "undesirable." A common example of this is the exclusion of multi-family dwellings which, in some areas, are seen as synonymous with low-income families and certain ethnic groups. This also extends to the NIMBY (not in my back yard) concept that is raised when group homes or residential therapeutic homes are seeking places to operate. —N.H.M.

The NIMBY (not in my back yard) phenomenon is challenging. For example, houses of worship are frequently considered undesirable neighbors and may find it difficult to locate themselves within a community. Sometimes the desires of individuals to control their neighborhoods should give way to the needs of the community. —D.E.

The ironically named "wise use movement," heavily funded by industry, seeks to sway public and legislative opinion away from regulation and toward inviolate individual and corporate property rights. This of course runs counter to a Jewish communitarian ethic, in which the Earth is God's . . . Mishna *Seder Nezikin,* the Order of Damages, is replete with examples of the community bearing indirect costs for economic production; over and over, our sacred texts give greater weight to the public good, while still trying to maximize private good as well. Public good almost always comes first, a priority we would do well to remember today. —F.S.D.

Criminal Actions

In general, actions that interfere with the safety of other persons or their possessions have been considered wrong throughout the long span of Jewish civilization whether such actions are accomplished directly or through agreements with others, whether by force or by guile. Such acts injure not only the person directly affected, but also those whose fortunes are intertwined with that person. They also damage the fabric of the community. When frequent, such acts can destroy the culture of the community and, ultimately, the community itself. They include murder; theft by deception, stealth or force; buying stolen goods; intentionally causing bodily harm; and committing sexual violations.

One exception to the prohibition against theft is if it is in service of a higher obligation that can be fulfilled in no other way. For example, saving a life by stealing food for a starving person is permitted if there is no other way to obtain the food.

Not everyone who commits a crime is caught, and the punishments for crimes differ from one locality to another, but the unethical nature of criminal activity remains unchanged. Intentionally inflicting bodily harm except as a defensive action, or damaging or gaining the property of another through force or deception are unethical actions.

This does not mean that people have unlimited property rights. These are constrained in several ways, such as

Bar and Bat Mitzva social events in congregations sometimes result in vandalism and damage to the building. It is a telling and depressing sign of the times that many congregations now routinely require congregants to hire security personnel to supervise such parties.   —R.H.

not having the right to interfere with the rights of others, and being subject to the community's right to impose taxes in order to serve the greater purposes of the group. This constraint on individuals' economic freedom is a natural consequence of the group's commitment to the welfare of the community as a whole.

Self-Defense

People have the right to defend themselves against criminal actions as long as the force employed is not excessive in relationship to the threat. Killing to save a life or to eliminate the criminal threat of physical violation is self-defense, and it is not considered an immoral act. Indeed, one has a positive obligation to protect oneself and preserve life (*pikuaḥ nefesh*), as well as the right to defend others and to protect oneself against unfair economic loss. One limitation on the claim to self-defense is that those committing crimes cannot ethically invoke such a claim when inflicting injury on innocent persons who are attempting to protect themselves.

Returning Lost Objects

In a society that emphasizes autonomy, people often say that they have no obligation to deal with problems they did not create. Judaism emphasizes community and therefore sees substantial mutual obligation. When someone finds an object and it is possible to identify the owner, for example, the finder has an obligation to return the object to its rightful owner (Deuteronomy 22:3). Keeping that object is a form of theft; leaving it where it lies is a lesser immoral act, but still wrong. When it is impossible to identify an owner—such as when a dollar bill is found lying in the street—the object can be claimed by the finder. When an object is found in a public place and the owner cannot be identified, it is considered *hefker,* ownerless property. Sometimes it is unclear whether ownership can be determined. In that case, the finder must make reasonable efforts to attempt to determine ownership.

When an animal is lost, the situation is not the same because an animal is not an object (Deuteronomy 22:1–4). *Tza'ar ba'aley ḥayim,* prevention of pain to animals, adds a dimension of obligation toward a lost animal, particularly if the lost animal could become distressed, injured, maltreated, or subjected to hunger or other adverse physical conditions (see Exodus 23:4–5). Thus two obligations exist that require returning an animal to its owner; however, *tza'ar ba'aley ḥayim* also means that one should not intentionally subject an animal to a situation where it is exposed to abuse.

Borrowing, Caretaking, and Damage

If a person borrows property and it becomes damaged while not in the owner's possession, the borrower must make up for the damage since the borrower benefited from having the object. This can mean reimbursing the owner for the full worth of the damaged object if it is beyond repair. On the other hand, if as a favor to the owner someone takes care of property and is not negligent with it, damage that occurs when it is not in the owner's possession comes at the expense of the owner since the owner was the beneficiary of the arrangement. If the owner pays the caretaker for watching the property at a location controlled by the caretaker, then the caretaker is liable for damage even if the caretaker is not negligent. Of course in all these cases, protection from some of the expense stemming from any of these liabilities can be afforded by purchasing appropriate insurance.

Ethical behavior requires that an owner disclose any existing damage when an object is borrowed or turned over to a caretaker. Similarly damage that occurs while the object is not in the owner's possession should be reported promptly to the owner. A fair assessment of the damage and allocation of the cost should follow. From a Jewish perspective, this is essentially not an adversarial situation, since both parties should want fairness for all concerned.

There are many other circumstances under which damages occur. When they are accidental, the person at fault simply pays for them; there is no further moral obligation. When the damages are intentional, this involves moral culpability that cannot fully be met by paying for the damages. This kind of culpability requires *t'shuva*, which involves several steps: offering apologies to everyone affected, making up for direct and indirect damages, and making a commitment never to repeat such actions. Attempting to conceal damages or avoid responsibility for one's role in creating damages is an unethical act.

One cannot just say "forget about it" when someone has suffered significant financial loss. That response diminishes the victim's self-respect and ignores the interactive nature of justice. —S.P.W.

If a person who causes injuries or property damage is not forthcoming in acknowledging responsibility and making fair recompense, the person who has sustained the damage has the moral right to pursue remedies to ensure repayment. If the person who has suffered the loss is underage or mentally incapacitated, that person's guardian or caretaker has a moral obligation to pursue recompense on that person's behalf.

Mediation, Arbitration, and Legal Judgments

When people have a dispute that they cannot resolve equitably on their own, they can turn to someone whom they both trust to mediate the dispute. Since mediation is the method most likely to reach an agreement that both parties believe is fair, it is the best next step.

If mediation fails or both parties will not agree to it, they can turn to arbitration. This may be done according to Jewish principles under the auspices of a *bet din* (a rabbinic court), but the parties should be informed that the outcome may well be different from one following civil legal principles, which differ in a variety of ways. If the parties agree to arbitration, it is important that they understand the principles that will be employed by the arbitrators and that they sign a legally binding agreement to abide by the arbitration decision before the process begins. It is

In another recognition of the rabbis' intelligent approach to practical ethics, it is worth mentioning that there is a clear trend in the United States today toward mediation and arbitration in place of litigation through the courts to settle disputes. —J.N.C.

the responsibility of arbitrators to ensure that such an agreement has been signed. One way that an arbitration panel can be selected is for each party to select one outside arbitrator, and for the two arbitrators to then pick a third.

If the parties do not agree to arbitration, which has the advantage of being less expensive and time-consuming as well as coming to a conclusion far sooner than legal proceedings, then the wronged party has the right to pursue a just outcome through the secular court system. In pre-modern times, Jews were admonished not to go to non-Jewish courts when the conflict was between Jews. This admonition developed because of fear of unfairness toward Jews in the non-Jewish courts and the fear of reinforcing anti-Semitism. In Western democratic nations where Jews are treated like all other citizens, this admonition is no longer relevant. In the absence of separate Jewish governance, it is reasonable for Jews to pursue secular, legal solutions. This follows the talmudic dictum, *dina d'malkhuta dina,* that Jews are bound by the secular law of their country.

Stumbling Blocks

One of the principles stated in the Torah is that one should not place a *mikhshol lifney iver,* a stumbling block before the blind (Leviticus 19:14). This principle has been greatly expanded over thousands of years of rabbinic interpretation. Using deception; employing coercion; or concealing information, motives or intentions are stumbling blocks that prevent their victims from discovering and acting in their own self-interest. They disrupt the cooperative relationships that are at the heart of a strong community.

The effort to remove the stumbling blocks in society that prevent access to justice involves acts of interpersonal kindness (*gemilut ḥesed*) and acts aimed at broader social change (*tikun olam*). These concepts are explored in another section of this *Guide*.

According to the rabbis, the Torah contains 365 "don'ts," and only 248 "do's." Ethical discussions like this one tend to focus on the negative formulations, bidding us to avoid known pitfalls more than promulgating forward-thinking guidelines for right conduct. So here in the home stretch, there is value in focusing for a moment on "the cooperative relationships that are at the heart of a strong community." Most of us, most of the time, do most things right (which is what enables most of us to enjoy the blessings of cooperative relationships and of strong communities, more often than not); we shouldn't lose sight of that. We should maintain a positive vision as we insert halakhic / legal "do's" and "don'ts" into an *aggadic* / narrative / values-based discussion of what the economy is for: community, equality of opportunity, sustainability, and sustaining the Spirit. —F.S.D.

For Further Reading

Dr. Leo Jung pioneered the modern study of Jewish business ethics. His book *Business Ethics in Jewish Law* was first published in the 1970s and has been reprinted several times since then. It remains a clear and useful introduction to the subject. Articles in *The Encyclopedia Judaica* on a variety of topics are useful in and of themselves and for their bibliographic references. There are several other popular books on business ethics. Those by Meir Tamari bring together sources spanning all periods and locales in a way that provides many insights into Jewish tradition. Tamari's first book, *With All Your Possessions: Jewish Ethics and Economic Life* (Free Press, 1987), is a broad survey.

Two more scholarly authors who have been prolific in their work on business ethics are Aaron Levine and Moses Pava, both of them professors at Yeshiva University. Levine's books include *Free Enterprise and Jewish Law* (KTAV, 1980), *Economics and Jewish Law* (KTAV, 1987), *Economic Public Policy and Jewish Law* (KTAV, 1993) and *Moral Issues of the Marketplace in Jewish Law* (Yashar Books, 2005). Pava wrote *Business Ethics: A Jewish Perspective* (KTAV, 1997). Pava and Levine jointly edited *Jewish Business Ethics: The Firm and its Stakeholders* (Jason Aronson, 1999).

Menaham Elon, a scholar and retired justice of the Israeli Supreme Court, wrote the invaluable *Mishpat Ivri,* a four-volume summary and analysis of Jewish law, which has appeared in English translation as *Jewish Law: History, Sources, Principles* (The Jewish Publication Society, 1994). Ed Zinbarg's *Faith, Morals, and Money* contains good comparisons of the business ethics found in Judaism with the ethics of other great religious traditions.

Biographies of Contributors

ADINA ABRAMOWITZ is the principal of Consulting for Change, a consulting practice specializing in maximizing the impact, market responsiveness and efficiency of community development nonprofits. She previously led the consulting and training program for the premier membership organization of Community Development Financial Institutions, Opportunity Finance Network, for ten years. She is a member of Dorshei Derekh, a Reconstructionist havurah in Philadelphia, and was a member of the Reconstructionist Prayerbook Commission.

JOSEPH COHEN is a graduate of Yale and Oxford universities who had a distinguished career as an investment banker on Wall Street, following which he redirected his efforts to Hollywood, where he was president of Largo Entertainment. Mr. Cohen currently advises a number of leading independent production companies and large international media concerns. He is also an adjunct professor at the Peter Stark Producing Program in the Graduate Film School of the University of Southern California.

RABBI FRED SCHERLINDER DOBB leads Adat Shalom Reconstructionist Congregation in Bethesda, MD.

RABBI DAN EHRENKRANTZ is the President of the Reconstructionist Rabbinical College. A past president of the Reconstructionist Rabbinical Association, he previously was rabbi of Congregation Bnai Keshet in Montclair, New Jersey.

RABBI RICHARD HIRSH is Executive Director of the Reconstructionist Rabbinical Association, a past editor of *The Reconstructionist,* and a former congregational rabbi. He teaches at the Reconstructionist Rabbinical College.

LEAH KAMIONKOWSKI is a certified public accountant. A vice president of the Jewish Reconstructionist Federation, she is a member of Kol HaLev in Cleveland, OH.

TAMAR KAMIONKOWSKI, Ph.D. is the Vice President for Academic Affairs and Associate Professor of Biblical Civilization at the Reconstructionist Rabbinical College.

RABBI MYRIAM KLOTZ teaches Torah, yoga and Jewish spirituality, leads retreats, and works in a variety of settings. She is on the staff of the Institute for Jewish Spirituality and faculty of Yedidya: Center for Jewish Spiritual Direction.

RABBI NINA H. MANDEL (RRC, 2003) serves Congregation Beth El in Sunbury, PA.

DEBORAH DASH MOORE is the Frederick G.L. Huetwell Professor of History at the University of Michigan and director of the Jewish studies program there. She is a member of the West End Synagogue in New York City.

MARK S. NUSSBAUM, CFP, CIMA, is a senior vice president for Investments with Wachovia Securities. Previously, Mark served as executive vice president and chief financial officer of PaineWebber Group, Inc., and as senior executive vice president and member of the board of directors of Western Federal Savings and Loan Association. Mark currently serves as a board member of the Reconstructionist Rabbincal College, and as a member of the endowment board of Congregation Dor Hadash in San Diego.

NANCY POST, a management consultant, executive coach and accupuncturist, has taught at the Wharton School and in Temple's Executive MBA program. She earned her Ph.D. in organizational behavior from the Union Institute and her MA and BA from the University of Pennsylvania. A member of the Jewish Reconstructionist Federation Board, she is an active member of Mishkan Shalom in Philadelphia.

RABBI YAEL RIDBERG is the rabbi of West End Synagogue in New York City.

LUIS SCHUCHINSKI retired as corporate vice president for taxes and insurance from Bestfoods, a multinational, branded grocery products company. He was born in Cuba, came to the United States in 1960 and received his J.D. degree in 1964 from the Yale Law School. He is a member of Congregation Bnai Keshet in Montclair, New Jersey.

RABBI JACOB STAUB is the Professor of Medieval Civilization at the Reconstructionist Rabbinical College, where he directs the program in Jewish Spiritual Direction. He previously served as its Vice President for Academic Affairs.

RABBI DAVID A. TEUTSCH is the Wiener Professor of Contemporary Jewish Civilization and Director of the Levin-Lieber Program in Jewish Ethics at the Reconstructionist Rabbinical College. A past president of the College, he was Editor-in-Chief of the *Kol Haneshamah* prayerbook series.

RABBI SHEILA PELTZ WEINBERG is Outreach Director and a staff member teaching meditation at the Institute for Jewish Spirituality. She has previously served as a congregational rabbi, Hillel director and community relations professional.

EDWARD D. ZINBARG retired as executive vice president of the Prudential Insurance Company. Previously he was director of Merrill Lynch (now BlackRock) mutual funds. He holds a Ph.D. in economics from New York University, an M.B.A. from the Wharton School, and an M.A. in religious ethics from Drew University. His most recent book is *Faith, Morals and Money: What the World's Religions Tell Us about Ethics in the Marketplace.*

Index